GERARD MANLEY
HOPKINS IN WALES

GERARD MANLEY HOPKINS IN WALES

NORMAN WHITE

Series Editor
John Powell Ward

seren

for Barbara Hardy

seren is the book imprint of
Poetry Wales Press Ltd
Wyndham Street, Bridgend, Wales

© Norman White, 1998
The moral right of Norman White to be identified
as the author of this work has been asserted

ISBN 1-85411-217-1 hbk
1-85411-218-X pbk

A CIP record for this title is available from the British Library

The publisher acknowledges the financial support of the
Arts Council of Wales

Cover: Gerard Hopkins, aged about 30

Printed in Palatino by WBC Book Manufacturers, Bridgend

Contents

List of Illustrations

Introduction

The person who most influenced Gerard Hopkins's writings was John Ruskin. In its anti-Catholicism and architectural description Hopkins's school-prize poem, 'The Escorial', closely resembles Ruskin's verse-criticism of Rheims Cathedral, written twenty-five years earlier but at almost the same age. As schoolboys both greatly admired – and continued to do so for the rest of their lives – George Herbert's poetic representation of Anglican theology, while being bored stiff with their local Anglican church: Ruskin found the Sunday services 'exhaust the little faith we have left' (*Praeterita*, III.1), while Hopkins wrote rude poems about the parson and imitated his pulpit mannerisms for his family's amusement. Having formed at school the intention of becoming a professional painter (as two of his brothers, Arthur and Everard, later did), in accordance with Ruskin's precepts and practices in *Modern Painters* Hopkins sketched and wrote journal descriptions of details in nature, particularly falling water, leaves and tree sprays, and wild flowers. His month's tour of Switzerland, his last artistic fling before joining the Society of Jesus, produced sketches in words and drawings of features Ruskin had drawn, all being done, as Hopkins said, 'in a Ruskinese point of view'.

Eventually, both Ruskin and Hopkins made 'the inevitable discovery of the falseness of the religious doctrines in which I had been educated' (not Hopkins's words, but Ruskin's, *Praeterita*, III.1); but whereas Hopkins, hemmed in by the personal guilt and scrupulousness encouraged by the constricting doctrines of 1860s Oxford, became a Roman Catholic, Ruskin, with a more wide-ranging mind, formed a dislike for 'Catholic political hierarchies', and continued to talk about 'pure religion' and 'the laws of God', while ceasing to be a practising Christian.

In spite of their divergence in formal religion, Ruskin and Hopkins continued to share a common enthusiasm for nature and an overwhelming desire to express their feelings about it. Refusing to deny the strong positive qualities in their responses to parts of nature, they both tried to validate their sensuous joy by insisting on its religious origin. According to contemporary puritanical dogma they had to justify their artistic works by emphasising their ethical value. And so Ruskin denied the validity of a pleasurable response to his writings – 'I don't care whether you enjoyed them; did they do you any good?' Many mid-Victorian artists had similar problems. Under the guise of stretching the boundaries of the moral world, both Ruskin and Hopkins substituted egoistic and sensuous joy ('I walk, I lift up, I lift up heart, eyes') for the old dogma that was closed (so they made out, with righteous indignation) to common-sense observation.

Ruskin diagnosed and faced this clash between moral and religious worlds:

> Having followed [the monk] for a time about the passages of the scattered building, in which there was nothing to show, – not a picture, not a statue, not a bit of old glass, or well-wrought vestment or jewellery; nor any architectural feature in the least ingenious or lovely, we came to a pause at last in what I suppose was a type of a modern Carthusian's cell, wherein, leaning on the window sill, I said something in the style of 'Modern Painters,' about the effect of the scene outside upon religious minds. Whereupon, with a curl of his lip, 'We do not come here,' said the monk, 'to look at the mountains.' Under which rebuke I bent my head silently, thinking however all the same, 'What then by all that's stupid, do you come here for at all?'
> (*Praeterita*, III.1)

But Hopkins never dealt adequately with the problem:

> The question then for me is not whether I am willing ... to make a sacrifice of hopes of fame ... but whether I am not to undergo a severe judgment from God for the lothness I have shewn in making it ... for the waste of time [my poems] ... may have

caused and their preoccupation of the mind which belonged to
more sacred or to more binding duties.
  (*L2*, 88, and see *White*, 334-5)

Poetry is a 'waste of time' and liable to 'severe judgment from God'.
Even letters to friends could be 'quite out of keeping with my present duties' (*L2*, 87). Renunciation and self-denial were virtues he
practised daily from well before he became a Jesuit; he gave up
painting because it was morally dangerous, and had to keep an
ever-watchful eye on poetry-writing. So whereas Ruskin can joyfully describe 'the mountain kingdom of which I claimed possession
by the law of love', Hopkins (just as much a compulsive writer) has
to have his Rector's sanction before he writes 'The Wreck of the
Deutschland', and is penalised for studying Duns Scotus, the dis-
credited philosopher who would be able to provide a line of argument which would justify Hopkins's pantheism.

  His period in Wales was of only three years, but, from the point
of view of the poet, they are the most important of his life. It is at St
Beuno's that Hopkins makes a serious break from his poetic silence
of almost seven years. 'The Wreck of the Deutschland' is the first
poem of his poetic maturity, and the story of its rejection gives the
reasons behind his subsequent withdrawal – for the rest of his life –
into the limiting form of the sonnet. St Beuno's is the main testing-
ground for his creativity, and for its relationship with his religious
vocation. It is also the place of his rare happy poems.

*   *   *

Parts of *Gerard Manley Hopkins in Wales* connected with the St Beuno's
locality and with Hopkins's use of the Welsh language originate in
work carried out for *Hopkins: A Literary Biography* (Clarendon Press,
1992, paperback Oxford University Press, 1995) but excluded from
the published book; the rest is new. To guard against the main commentary on the major poems Hopkins wrote in 1876-77, chapters six
('The Wreck of the Deutschland') and nine (the 1877 sonnets), echoing the reactions printed in the St Beuno's section of the biography,
I looked at the poetry afresh, ignoring anything I had written before.
In the case of 'The Wreck of the Deutschland' the focus changed to

the shipwreck in the mouth of the Thames: how it was reported in 1875 and Hopkins's highly selective response to those reports, while the 1877 sonnets are in this study closely tied in with the emotional and professional circumstances of Hopkins's final year at St Beuno's College. The idea for chapter four, 'The Year at Saint Beuno's', came when I was talking to people whose families had lived continuously in the area from before Hopkins's time.

* * *

I am particularly grateful to Nest Price for help with chapters four and eight, and for letting me draw on her knowledge and understanding of the St Beuno's locality. John Powell Ward has been a considerate editor. I acknowledge with thanks a grant from the Faculty of Arts Academic Fund, University College, Dublin. Chapter eight originally appeared in *The Hopkins Quarterly* in a slightly different form, and I thank the editors for permitting me to reprint it here. The author and publishers are grateful to the following for permission to reproduce the following illustrations: Frontispiece, Humanities Research Center, University of Texas at Austin; 3, 4, 11, 12, the Archives of the British Province, Society of Jesus; 2, 8, 9, 13, 14, the Alfred Thomas SJ collection, currently in the Archives of the British Province, Society of Jesus; 10, County Archivist, Flintshire Record Office. Other photographs by the author.

One
'To seem the stranger lies my lot':
Hopkins the Borderer

Gerard Hopkins was born on 28 July 1844. His second name, Manley, was his father's first name and his grandmother's surname, after the mid-Devonshire hamlet where she was born; but it was seldom used by Gerard or those who knew him during his lifetime. He was known by everyone as Gerard (or sometimes Gerry) Hopkins from his birth until 1918, almost thirty years after his death, and so that is what he will be called in this work. It was only in 1918 that the name 'Gerard Manley Hopkins' first appeared, on the title-page of the first edition of his *Poems*. In that year, the Poet Laureate Robert Bridges, who had been given the task of editing the largely unknown and unpublished poetry of his dead friend, decided to ignore the name he knew and preferred ('Gerard Hopkins') and substitute the longer form, partly as a compliment to Hopkins's dead father, and partly to distinguish him from the son born in 1892 to Everard, Gerard's youngest brother, who had been named after his dead uncle.

To judge from the wide cultural interests he later showed as a pater familias, Manley, Gerard's father, would have benefited from a university education. But Manley's father, Martin Hopkins, had died tragically in early middle age, almost bankrupt, having failed as a commodity speculator, leaving penniless a widow and young family; and so Manley had had to leave school in 1832, when he was only fourteen, to take a job in the City of London. But Manley had worked assiduously in an insurance-office specialising in marine law. In 1843 he had married the daughter of a fashionable and wealthy doctor, Kate Smith, who had been brought up in a comfortable and relaxed way of life in Trinity Square, by the Tower of London; and by the time his first child, Gerard, was born in the following year, Manley had already set up his own firm of average adjusters, the professionals who, after a shipwreck, divided losses and expenses among the underwriters.

On his marriage, Manley had set up his household at Stratford, in Essex, just outside the eastern boundary of London, and Gerard spent his first eight years there. Stratford had been Martin's home town in happier days before venturing into the City, and by returning there Manley was proclaiming that his hard work had restored the family's financial and social standing. (His marriage to Kate Smith, a plain young lady with coarse features, but with money and comparatively higher and certainly more secure rank, was another part of this restorative process.) Manley developed an amateur interest in genealogy and adopted enthusiastically the coat-of-arms his father had occasionally used, one of doubtful authenticity and inept construction (he used the crest alone, of a tower on fire, as though it were the whole coat of arms), but which, printed or embossed on fine note-paper, suggested a long and noble family tradition, rather than recent near-disaster and nose-to-grindstone recovery.

In Martin Hopkins's day Stratford had been a rural retreat for gentlefolk, a tranquil pastoral escape for City businessmen, but industrialisation had overtaken it fast, in the shape of factories, offensive trades banned from London, and the railway; within sight and sound of the Hopkins home in The Grove was a vast network of dirty and noisy railway sidings. Cholera, which had killed some of Kate's close relatives when she was a girl, was now, in the eighteen-forties and -fifties, raging once again in the neighbourhood. The family needed an up-to-date retreat, pastoral yet within easy reach of the City of London. Manley's business was flourishing and they could afford to move.

So in 1852 the Hopkins family – Manley, Kate, their four children, Gerard, Cyril, Arthur, and Milicent, and Manley's mother and sister Ann – moved to Hampstead, a prosperous, generously laid-out, semi-rural village, on a northern hill near London, but separated from it and its yellow fogs by its height and by Hampstead Heath, a few hundred undeveloped acres of woods, grasslands, avenues and ponds. The new Hopkins home, a modern, large and comfortable house, aesthetically innocuous, but with a large garden and developed trees, was one of a spacious group of semi-detached 'gentlemen's dwellings', which had won a prize in the 1851 Great Exhibition. Their neighbours were comfortably middle-class, all with live-in servants, and some with their own carriage, though the Hopkinses never attained this status-symbol, using as excuse the proximity of a mews almost opposite their house on Oak Hill Park. The Hopkins males could all ride, Manley sometimes hiring a horse to ride to work; otherwise they were well provided with transport, horse-trams being a five-minute walk away in the Bird-in-Hand yard, in the centre of Hampstead, and the new trains only ten minutes. By Victorian standards, even central London was within walking distance.

Gerard was brought up with the fortunate benefits of a comfortable and prosperous home almost in the countryside, yet able to avail himself of all the wide variety of sophisticated educational, social and aesthetic amenities offered by the capital city of the world's most developed nation. Within easy reach were the new London public museums and art galleries, parks and squares, theatres, elegant shops, political and other meetings, church and cathedral services and the doctrinal arguments they provoked, ecclesiastical architecture both old and provocatively modern, a variety of streets, military spectacles, Parliament itself, traditional ceremonial rubbing shoulders with the latest political and social events, a general air of being at the centre of the most important goings-on.

Although aesthetically and educationally amenable in many ways, Hampstead also meant for Gerard petty restrictions of intellect and society imposed by his unsophisticated family (soon enlarged to five boys and three girls). His father's interests were wide, but Manley rarely progressed beyond the elements of a subject; the contents of his library and his writings show that he was easily satisfied, seldom being puzzled or asking difficult questions, before turning to another subject for enthusiastic skimming. Manley's seriousness would often tail off into whimsicality or unctuousness, a characteristic made fun of by his eldest son, who developed a gift for mimicry. Kate's family, the Smiths of Trinity Square, had been late in adapting to the new age of periodicals and everyday reading, and brought up in a largely oral culture she does not seem to have been active in educating her children, who, after her death had difficulty in describing her mental nature.

Manley's sister Ann was Gerard's governess for a time, but although she busied herself in books on archaeology and other subjects she did not command the boy's respect, and the extant portraits which she painted of him as an angelic choirboy suggest an unreal attitude. From infancy, Gerard Hopkins was a voracious reader, fastening on details while exploring a wide range of contemporary branches of learning into depths beyond the inclination and capacity of his family at Oak Hill. He needed and took advantage of formal education much more than any of his four brothers; he was the only one who went to a university, although Manley's increasing business success meant that the family could have afforded the expense. Sir Roger Cholmondley's school at Highgate was not an eminent public school, but its old-fashioned syllabus, which focused on the classics for an abnormally large proportion of its teaching time, gave Hopkins a solid background and fluency in the mechanics of language and poetry. In the sixth form he made an enemy of the headmaster and ceased being a boarder, having to walk every day across the Heath and back, but nevertheless he won his school's Exhibition, an award tenable at Oxford or Cambridge, and also, at his second attempt, a house Exhibition at Balliol College, Oxford.

Hopkins's final evaluation of Highgate school was of its headmaster, Dr Dyne, whom he called 'the Old Dispensation'; education there was the dispensing of Old Knowledge, not the New discovered and self-explored. Hopkins took what he wanted from Highgate, but neither his personality nor his interests narrowly conformed to its conventions; some of his schoolboy photographs show a scruffy, defiant persona, with arrogant, arched eyebrows. The school's deficiencies gave him touchstones for many cultural dissatisfactions, which would be properly tested and worked out only at Oxford.

Gerard Hopkins's school-days were not the happiest of his life. Everything up to now had been a preparation for Oxford, where for the first time in his life the reality seemed ideal. Everything Oxonian provoked him – people, social life, arguments, nature, architecture, reading within and outside the university syllabus. His four years at Oxford, from 1863 to 1867, was a time of self-discovery; his being was made there, he admitted several years later. There were close friendships, and the best liberal education of the day, personified in two of his Balliol teachers, the eminent scholars Benjamin Jowett, the Regius Professor of Greek, and the philosopher T.H. Green. Even Oxford's religion suited him; he found richness, seriousness, and intense debate, which he could participate in and legitimately connect with many sorts of exciting aesthetic and personal indulgences and puritanisms.

But from the outset of his time at Oxford Hopkins came under the influence of the fashionable High Church preachers, Canon H.P. Liddon and Dr E.B. Pusey, who (though they strenuously denied it) had been the final stepping-stones of many undergraduates on the path from the Church of England to Roman Catholicism. Whereas Hopkins had been brought up in an easy-going, moderately high version of Anglicanism, he had shown no admiration for the family church of St John's, Hampstead, which he called 'dreary', in spite of its generously lit eighteenth-century windows, or for its preachers, whose pulpit gestures he had imitated to amuse his brothers and sisters. In 1860s Oxford it was difficult for young men to avoid deeply morbid and closely puritanical religious dogmatising, and the powerfully dramatic rhetoric and severe message of the Oxford ritualists had a strong effect on Hopkins. He started austere religious practices which to most Anglicans seemed to belong to the Roman Catholic church: fasting, self-inflicted punishment, kissing the floor in front of an effigy of the Virgin Mary in his college room, going to confession, and making a detailed daily note of his sins. The High Church Ritualists were especially puritanical about personal sexual morality (Pusey is known to have advised circumcision for girls who masturbated), and Hopkins became trapped in a behavioural scrupulosity which enmeshed him for the rest of his life.

After a short time at Oxford he discarded the idea he had held for some years of wanting to be a professional painter, on the grounds that such a career would dangerously inflame his passions. There are no extant paintings that Hopkins did after the age of ten, but several sketches survive that he drew as a late adolescent, following the precepts of the fashionable writer on nature and art, John Ruskin, of countryside scenes, details of plants and hedgerows, and of architectural tracery. With the odd exception, these are not completed pictures but illustrations of observations about nature and architecture, of the kind with which he filled his diaries while he was at Oxford. In an age when many middle-class people sketched on picnics or in the parlour, Hopkins's drawings are not outstanding, and show that he probably had an exaggerated idea of his abilities in this field; a comparison with the contemporary sketchbooks of his younger brother Arthur reveals that at least one of his brothers was more gifted.

The most fascinating writings of his at Oxford were his notebooks. He often used the observations he made about natural sights and etymological conjectures and peculiarities in his conventional and dull undergraduate poems. He also made in his notebooks pseudo-scholarly lists of words whose sound demonstrated their meaning and which he would use throughout his poetic career, together with lists of similar-sounding words whose meanings were also apparently associated. His academic studies at Oxford and his own explorations and experiments formed a valuable apprenticeship for a poet, though the poetry he wrote at Oxford is largely imitative and unexciting.

Early in 1865, soon after meeting Digby Dolben, an Eton schoolboy of extravagant religious and poetic tastes and behaviour, Hopkins's daily confessional notes reveal his increasing self-dissatisfaction and his moving further away from the Anglican church. His spiritual barrenness was relieved by reading Newman's account of his advance towards Rome in the *Apologia Pro Vita Sua*, published in 1864, and he expressed his own religious conflicts in several poems, some of which, such as 'The Half-Way House', borrow

Newman's images. Influenced by Dolben he vowed to 'give up beauty', in a typical romantic gesture, but shortly afterwards felt compelled to continue describing nature. Unable to come to terms with his own temperament he felt increasingly the necessity for a stronger religious model to correct and control him.

In October 1866 Hopkins was received into the Roman Catholic church by Newman, and in April the next year he took a first-class degree. At Newman's invitation he became a resident master at the Oratory School, Birmingham, but he was unhappy in the post, complaining of mental fatigue, overwork, lack of newspapers and contact with current events, and being allowed too little time to follow his own interests; all of these reactions to his first teaching post anticipate complaints he would often voice during his professional religious career. In common with contemporary religious psychology, he thought that the remedy for depression lay in a tightening of discipline. In April 1868 he went on a retreat to the Jesuit Manresa House, at Roehampton; halfway through he resolved to write no more verse and to destroy what he had written, and at the end of the retreat decided to be a professional religious, either a Benedictine or a Jesuit. He burned all his poems, though it was only another romantic gesture; it turned out later that he had sent copies of all of them to his friend Robert Bridges, and only three months afterwards he described enthusiastically in a letter the new beat he had introduced into his verse.

At the end of an invigorating walking holiday in Switzerland, of which he wrote a marvellous account in his journal, using the new words 'inscape' and 'instress', in September 1868 Hopkins entered the Jesuit novitiate at Manresa House, Roehampton. An early clash between his old habits and the new habit of perfection occurred when, to his surprise, he was forbidden to keep with him Swinburne's *Poems and Ballads*. Hopkins was by nature a compulsive writer, and by January 1869 he was writing confidently, though sporadically, in his secular journal, mainly about sunsets and weather-effects. In September 1870 he took his vows as a Jesuit scholastic, and was posted for three years of 'Philosophy' to St Mary's Hall, at Stonyhurst, a large parkland estate at the tip of the Forest of Bowland, in the Lancashire millstone moors. After two years at Roehampton, the noviceship had seemed to him a second home; Stonyhurst was not just strange but extremely rainy, and several letters of his over the next three years sound the same note of pessimism and complaint against the wintry climate and sparseness of fine weather. But once spring started his journal comes to life with joyful natural descriptions and records of extraordinary atmospheric and climatic occurrences.

In spite of his previous denunciation of poetry because it 'wd. interfere with my state and vocation', at Stonyhurst Hopkins wrote two poems in honour of the Virgin Mary, as seminarians were encouraged to do on the first of May, but neither of them rose above the standards of a dutiful exercise. More importantly for his later poetic practice, he used his journal on two holidays at Douglas, in the Isle of Man, to describe vivid and intense seascapes, which convey his extraordinary excitement at and analytic perceptions of waves and shore. After his second Isle of Man holiday in August 1873, Hopkins was given a rest by his superiors, and set out for Roehampton again, to teach Classics and English to junior scholastics for one year before proceeding to his theology training. He taught only in mornings and evenings, and had Thursdays and Sundays completely free. He made full use of Roehampton's proximity to London, visiting his family at Hampstead and going round the capital's museums, galleries and exhibitions, even attending an occasional trial, and he renewed contact with several old friends, including Robert Bridges. But teaching never suited him, and he became tired and depressed. A holiday in South Devon in summer 1874 renewed his vitality and interest in nature, and he was ready to start his four-year course of theology, which was to take place at St Beuno's in North Wales. He was now thirty years old.

* * *

It would not be until ten years later, after many more journeys and changes and disappointments and failures, when he had arrived in Dublin, on his last melancholy and unsuitable posting, that he would formulate a summary of his life as a Borderer: 'To seem the stranger lies my lot, my life / Among strangers'. But by the time his train puffed over the River Dee into Wales on 28 August 1874,

Hopkins had already crossed several frontiers of a more elusive kind, and was someone without a conventional identity, who inhabited a region of uncertain allegiances, of antitheses.

A person of highly individual reactions and pursuits, he had made a habit of not accepting or settling within the secure conventions of any geographical or ideological location, always being on the edge of a territory and trying to elasticise its boundaries. From an early age he was an outsider in the Hopkins family, determined to go beyond their limitations, and not acknowledging the material and emotional security which he had fortunately been born into. Yet when he discarded the Oak Hill familial intimacy and stability for the calculated formality of a large religious organisation, where insecurity of personal and local relationships was encouraged in the cause of a greater, disciplined duty, he experienced the lonely, sentimental longing of the institutionalised for human warmth and relationships.

A rebel at his Highgate school, his antagonism towards its brand of regimentation nearly cost him the award which enabled him to enter the more powerful and congenial world of Oxford. There, for the first and only time in his life, he found himself among intellectual equals and constant mental and sensuous stimulation; he developed mental characteristics which were recognisably Oxonian, and which stayed with him for the rest of his life. But again he refused easy conformity, rebelling against the advanced but unsettling Balliol philosophical ethos, and allying himself with the broken but more comprehensive religious tradition of medieval England, in the post-Reformation version of J.H. Newman. His sceptical teacher, the eminent philosopher T.H. Green, described Hopkins's stance as heroic but painful, characterising him as 'one of those who ... instead of simply opening themselves to the revelation of God in the reasonable world, are fain to put themselves into an attitude'. Hopkins was a modern 'superior young man', who 'hugs his own "refined pleasures" or ... his personal sanctity'. By choosing to serve the 'exceptional institution' of the Society of Jesus, said Green, Hopkins had wilfully placed himself 'in opposition to loyal service to society', and his 'fine nature' would be 'victimised' by the Jesuit system.

A genius at individuality, Hopkins had made himself subservient to a regimented organisation which controlled its members' bodies and minds for every minute of the day, where individual behaviour was frowned on, and where imagination and the senses had to be harnessed within a specific dogmatic syllabus. An original institutionalised among soldiers who prized orthodoxy, he remained a poetic thinker among prosaic activists. He became known as an 'eccentric', even a 'joker' and 'clown', among the serious. He developed deep responses to non-orthodox subjects and areas. He read Matthew Arnold in the recreation room, while the others were repeating jokes from the local newspaper, and wrote while around him billiards was being played. He came to side with the Franciscan rebel and misunderstood genius, Duns Scotus, against Aquinas, the approved conventional Dominican, whose teachings represented to the Jesuits the orthodox theology of the day.

He had changed from being a Romanist-inclined Anglican to a Roman Catholic who retained Anglican and Protestant influences. Another unstable factor was his locality, now that he could no longer call Oak Hill his home. As a Jesuit he always had to be prepared to pack his bags and travel to any part of Britain at a moment's notice. 'Permanence with us is ginger-bread permanence', he wrote to Bridges, 'cobweb, soapsud, and frost-feather permanence' (*L1*, 55). Saint Ignatius had considered that his company's prime operating bases would be in towns, so that Hopkins could have counted himself fortunate that most of his postings would be as a teacher in rural or semi-rural surroundings. He spent a total of only two years (1879-81) as curate in working-class areas of industrial towns with large numbers of Catholic immigrants, but was unable to repress his horror at the conditions of the people and places he encountered. While living at Hampstead he had become familiar with the amenities of the more prosperous parts of public central London, but had remained at a middle-class distance from its tucked-away rookeries and slums. In his Lancashire and Glasgow parishes he appeared as an impractical Oxford-educated southerner, and even when curate in the new church at Oxford (1878-79) was unable to mix satisfactorily with parishioners of a lower class.

Often too he was an English outsider in largely Celtic Jesuit communities, sometimes staffed by exiled teachers who did not speak

English as their native tongue. His ultimate unfortunate polarisation was as a strict law-abiding Englishman in rebellious Ireland of the eighteen-eighties, an extreme situation which made permanent his previously intermittent melancholia, and hastened his premature death (June 1889). He did not have the natural strength that Newman possessed to overcome exile and other blows of fate; he constantly needed mental cushions. He was always the stranger, the outsider in several senses. He never achieved a satisfactory general state of body and mind, which may be the main reason why his grand generalisations are seldom convincing; unconsciously he seems to have cultivated the instability which his writing genius needed in order to breathe.

Two
'On a hillside of the beautiful valley of the Clwyd': Saint Beuno's

On Friday 28 August 1874 Hopkins travelled to St Beuno's College, in North Wales, to study theology for four years. He rose at half-past four from his bed at Manresa House, Roehampton; he noticed that there was still a full moon, of 'brassyish colour and beautifully dappled' (J, 257), hanging just above the clump of trees in the pasture opposite his bedroom window.

From London it is most likely that he caught the Irish Mail, or 'The Wild Irishman', as it was popularly known, part of the London and North-Western system, and one of the finest lines of railway in the kingdom. The train crossed the Thames Valley, through the Chiltern Hills to Oxford; over the river Avon, then through the South Midlands into the Black Country, and on to Chester, where it passed under part of the ancient city, on to the Chester and Holyhead Railway. Then across the Dee, and the train was in Wales, branching right at Saltney from the Great Western Railway.

Hopkins could see in the distance the mountain Moel Fammau, highest of the Clwydian range, and Hawarden Church where Mr Gladstone worshipped, and the trees of the park, before passing Queen's Ferry. The railway track then skirted the broad but shallow estuary of the River Dee on his right, while Hopkins's view to the left was limited by the hills which descended nearly to the water's edge, leaving no more than a narrow strip of uncertain sand to bear the rails. Then on his right the ruins of Edward I's Flint Castle, with its free-standing great tower, and the ugly collection of lead-smelting works and dwelling-houses which formed Flint. In a few moments the train reached Bagillt, with another smoky smelting-mill, the line here running almost into the water, and so giving a good view of the widening estuary. Five minutes more, and he could glimpse the ruins of the once rich and magnificent Cistercian Abbey of Basingwerk, amongst the trees on a gentle eminence to the left, near a lofty chimney and the junction of a mineral line with the main railway.

The train stopped at Holywell Junction, and then Mostyn Quay. The track bent left by the Point of Ayr lighthouse, and afterwards on his left appeared one of the white stations of the old semaphore system which had connected the North Welsh coast with Liverpool, and which had been used before the days of the telegraph to announce the arrival of ships. Then the developing village of Prestatyn, with its straggling main street, newly erected dwelling-houses, tall chimneys of the alkali works, and still largely unreclaimed foreshore, though there were already a few pioneer bathing-machines. Out of Prestatyn the hills began to recede, and soon he found that the train was crossing a nearly level plain after a gentle rise from the sea. As the train approached Rhyl, in front were the Great Orme's Head and Penmaen-mawr, and the first glimpse of the greater mountains: Carnedd Llewelyn, and the long range of which it is the highest point. On the left was again Moel Fammau, and the scanty ruins of Dyserth Castle standing out on the summit of a green hill.

At the rapidly rising watering-place of Rhyl, proud of its spruce new pier, Hopkins stepped onto the long platform to change to a train of the new branch-line Vale of Clwyd Railway, and his train-journey finished when he got out at the little town of St Asaph. There was a St Beuno's pony and trap to meet him; in it were a Mr Bodoano, whom he did not know, and an old friend, Henry Schomberg Kerr, who had been one year ahead of him in the novitiate at Roehampton. The trap turned away from the small neat brick houses of the town under the railway-bridge into the Chester to Holywell road, and immediately there were fields on both sides. As they descended the hill just beyond the station Hopkins saw in front of him the slender River Clwyd prettily meandering away into the distance. The trap crossed the river at the old cobbled Pont Dafydd Esgob (Bishop David's bridge), and on his left he saw the brick farmhouse Rhyllon, in which, some fifty years earlier, had lived the popular poetess Mrs Felicia Hemans, author of 'Casabianca' ('The boy stood on the burning deck').

Past meadows edged with masses of dark trees, and small rich green or yellow fields with grazing sheep and cattle, the occasional group of three or four low rough-stone farm-buildings, such as Pant Evan, a mile out of St Asaph, occasional woods and corn-fields ripe for harvesting, the almost straight road climbed gently for a mile; the sea-bay gradually appeared over the rooftops of Rhyl in the left-distance, and the dense dark-wooded Clwydian Hill range stretching across the skyline in front of the trap drew nearer. Then the road wound and the range divided into two long hills: one comprised Y Foel (the bare hill) and Mynydd y Cwm (Cwm mountain), and the other was Moel Maenefa, the bare hill Maenefa (Maenefa meaning 'the stony place').

Round a bend up Rhuallt Hill, beyond Glan yr Afon (River-Bank), one of the valley's rare three-storied houses, they suddenly came upon the Rhuallt crossroads, amid a small cluster of houses and the Smithy Arms among trees, and the corn-mill visible down the side-road to Cwm. The main road disappeared over a hill into woods, but the trap turned right, by a Methodist chapel and its adjoining British School, on to a narrow and uneven road, frequently splattered with cow and horse dung; up another bending hill, then steeply down, with Maenefa looming above over black trees on their left, and on the right, over bramble hedgerows, grass, weeds, and a variety of yellow and magenta wild flowers, was a view gently down over a field-patchwork of green rectangles into the river valley; and across the valley to clear hills and vaguer mountain-ranges beyond – it was difficult to say how many.

A drive by a gatehouse led to a tree-mass and a large house Pistyll above the now gentle road, level on the edge of the valley; across a shallow stream, the old farm-buildings of Ty Gwyn (the White House) were now below to their right, and above to the left Maenefa's summit now distinct and seemingly near. Crows circled a small group of trees on a long mound: the Welsh border-country drove-roads carried great concentrations of Scots pines planted in clumps 'to mark the way and signal where grazing and hospitality could be had for the night' (*Flora*, 23). Here the carriage veered left, climbing steeply a narrow and muddy winding track, with a stream running beside it. Ahead the land rose steeply into the wide bare hill of Maenefa, whose summit formed a high uneven horizon. Beyond a dense hedgerow of innumerable varieties of plants, intermingling holly and brambles, with sparse blackberries ready to pick, the carriage veered sharply right between gate-posts into a mass of trees.

The St Beuno's College drive wound up to the stables, but straight on was the main courtyard and college entrance, and Hopkins was soon staring at the buildings on three sides, deeply hidden by vegetation from the road, and with all the walls severely constructed in irregular rows of white limestone blocks, with pigeon-grey slate roofs. His trunk was unloaded, and the trap driven around to the stables. On his left was a long low nondescript domestic building, with a dark gateway and stagey wooden portcullis near the far end; beyond that its windows were heavily leaded in diamond-patterns, meeting similarly leaded arched windows in the buttressed wall of the gothic refectory facing him. To the right was the main, more elaborate building of three domestic-gothic stories, the lowest of which was below ground-level. It had five steep and cramped gables, the central one jutting over the main door, its gas-light showing shallow stone steps curving down to the courtyard. To the right of the steps, where Hansom and Son's workmen had only just completed the new extension, the colour of the stone noticeably changed.

Looking upward he saw on the skyline what he later called 'a medley of ricks and roofs and dovecots', triangles and rectangles and chimney-pots, a miscellaneous jumble of architectural bits and pieces, all crowded on the steep hillside plateau. A path rolled steeply down to a lower terrace, the bright Broad Walk, bordered with stone-urns planted with flowers.

Other familiar faces now appeared and welcomed Hopkins to St Beuno's. First there was William Hobart Kerr, who, like his younger brother Henry, was about to start his second year of theology, and had been with Hopkins and Henry at Roehampton. Then there was Francis Edward Bacon, who had also been in the novitiate at Manresa House with Hopkins, but a year ahead of him in studies. Hopkins went up the steps, in at a wooden door within a larger gothic one panelled in blue, red and yellow stained glass, and found himself in a low ten-feet-wide corridor, the Main Gallery, with diamond windows overlooking the courtyard on one side, and dark arched pitchpine doors on the other; a blue and gilt statue of the Virgin Mary and Child was at one end, and the floor was patterned in diamonds and zigzags of dull red, black and cream tiles. He reported to the Minister, Father Murphy, the house's administrator, and was shown upstairs to his own room, where he was touched to see – as well as the dark prie-dieu and its cushion, two tables and a chair, an iron bedstead with crucifix above and charley (or chamber-pot) beneath, a chest of drawers, inkwell, candle and wax taper, mat, mirror, wash-basin, jug and towel – some bright scarlet geraniums, which Francis Bacon had picked for him from the many that flourished on both sides of the numerous flights of stony steps leading up through the college's steep gardens. Hopkins's room was probably a light and spacious one in Hamlets or Mansions Gallery, with a view either from magnificently high over the Clwyd valley, or a more subdued but still interesting one upwards over the gardens on the hill, beyond trees to Maenefa's summit.

Hopkins felt that everyone was very kind and hospitable. He would be shown the refectory (English Jesuits emphasized the first syllable, a relict of the Latin word and pronunciation), the chapel, w.c.s, and the one bath. This had to do for the whole community of sixty or so, a hygienic puritanism which was to affect his health for the rest of his life. Later, he reported to his new Rector, Fr James Jones, whom he already knew from the annual retreat given two years before at St Mary's Hall Stonyhurst, when Hopkins was a second-year Philosopher.

* * *

Beuno, a seventh-century Celtic saint whose life, says Alban Butler, is a 'most fantastic narrative which merits no confidence', was an itinerant founder of monasteries and builder of churches in North

Wales, where he became the counterpart of St David in the south. In North Wales one still occasionally comes across the occasional church dedicated to St Beuno, such as at Clynnog-fawr, on the north coast of the Lleyn Peninsula, where there is also his stone. He was inseparably connected with his presumed niece, St Winefride, whose well at Holywell was the great shrine in the north of Wales, and the only place of pilgrimage in Britain whose Roman Catholic history remained unbroken by the Reformation. Holywell, on the Dee estuary, had housed the lone permanent representative of the Society of Jesus in Wales from 1679 until 1848. In that year St Beuno's College was established as the theologate or divinity school for scholastics, on a site sufficiently secluded to discourage common informers from invoking the anti-Jesuit laws, in the parish of Tremeirchion, a tiny village eight and a half miles inland, west of Holywell.

Holywell had been the furthest east that the cult of Beuno had established itself, whereas Tremeirchion was set solidly in Beuno-cult country, with its own Ffynnon Beuno (Beuno's Well) and Ffynnon Beuno Inn. Besides housing the theologate the college had sent out missions into nearby towns such as Denbigh, Rhyl, Saint Asaph and Ruthin, which were served by Jesuit fathers until the parishes were sufficiently established to hand over to local secular clergy. St Beuno's, then, was an appropriate name for an institution of Catholic missionaries in that part of Great Britain, but its Celtic name also revealed wishful thinking. It was in the heart of the Welsh-speaking area which Beuno had known, but which was now staunchly Low Church; and yet it was largely manned by English-speaking Jesuits of the English Province. (A local priest told me that St Beuno's was sometimes known in the district as 'the College of Englishmen'.)

* * *

Having been a teacher for the previous year Hopkins was about to become a student again. But classes did not begin until October, and now most of the community were on holiday at Barmouth, on the west coast of Wales; and the Rector himself would be away giving a retreat at Beaumont from the following day, Saturday. Hopkins had then five weeks largely to himself, in which to explore the surrounding countryside and accustom himself to the almost deserted college, with its skeleton staff.

He found the main building formed in low-ceilinged corridors or 'galleries', ten feet wide and fifty yards long. These surrounded two small square courtyards, one the entrance court, and the other a hidden rose-garden. Most galleries had a straightforward name, like the Main Gallery, or Basement Gallery, or Priests' Gallery, or Chapel Gallery, or Infirmary Gallery; but others had acquired esoteric names in their twenty-five year history, like Hamlets, or Mansions, or Attica, or Bacon Lane. Each gallery had its distinctive quality, usually associated with the functions of its rooms. The Main Gallery held professors' rooms and the Fathers' recreation-room in the recently completed extension, and in the original half of that gallery was the Bishop's room, more elaborately decorated and expensively furnished than any other in the house, and kept for receptions of distinguished visitors. The Basement Gallery was paved with massive stone flags in twos and threes, like bonded brickwork, for half its length, until uneven and disfigured flags by the old Tower entrance in the centre showed where the new extension to the west wing had recently been completed; the flags in the new part were new but smaller, in threes and fours. Feet and voices made a deeper longer echo in that gallery. The sparse natural light slanted in through high windows from the courtyards above, though when a door opened on the west-facing side of the gallery, brilliant light streamed from the Broad Walk gardens across the dark corridor. It had new large lecture-rooms and so fewer doors than other corridors. Each gallery was distinguished by statues or pictures of its particular saints, and some were divided by a carved gothic wooden screen.

With its logical structure it should have been easy to discover one's way about the house, but newcomers did not find it so. Any explanation of how to get to a particular distant room usually only led to confusion, the essential staircases being hidden behind doors looking like room doors. 'The staircases, galleries, and bopeeps are inexpressible', Hopkins wrote to his father on Saturday, 'it takes a fortnight to learn them' (*L3*, 124). The stranger in an almost empty house could easily get lost on isolated landings, or find himself in a nook built into the roof-gables, or suddenly emerging into the middle of a vast gallery.

The Pugin-inspired architecture of the college did not interest Hopkins: it was 'decent outside, skimpin within, Gothic', not pure or elaborate enough for him, and derivative at that. It had been designed by the inventor of the horse-cab, Joseph Hansom, who was responsible for many of the architecturally undistinguished buildings Hopkins lived in as a Jesuit. The part of St Beuno's which most aroused his enthusiasm was its steep gardens. He wrote:

> The garden is all heights, terraces, Excelsiors [further and further on upwards], misty mountain tops, seats up trees called Crows' Nests, flights of steps seemingly up to heaven lined with burning aspiration upon aspiration of scarlet geraniums: it is very pretty and airy but it gives you the impression that if you took a step farther you would find yourself somewhere on Plenlimmon, Conway Castle, or Salisbury Craig.
> (L3, 124-5)

From the top walk, or terrace, parallel with the long-drawn valley of the Clwyd and with the river itself, was a vast prospect across to a line of wood-covered hills, with a range of higher hills or mountains apparently just behind that; a further range beyond that, and behind was the Snowdonian range, which, as Hopkins wrote, was sometimes 'bright visible but coming and going with the weather'. Garden seats in shallow stone alcoves off the highest terrace all faced these ranges, which complemented the Clwydian range on the eastern, St Beuno's side of the vale; Maenefa looked across to the cloud-mists of Snowdon.

So steep was the incline of Maenefa that from the highest garden terrace Hopkins was almost on a level with the tallest of the college's tall chimneys. To someone looking down on the jumble of towers, thrusting ornaments, gables, chimneys, and pots, there were no horizontals, all steep grey-blue slate diagonals and white limestone verticals, jammed together, like an illustration of a medieval city, except that no ground-plan seemed evident. There was an uneasy Victorian mix of primitive and sophisticated. The architect seemed to fear a continuous horizontal line, to resist which he had thrust out unusual prominent chimneys or gables or attics, or arches or tall rectangular windows. The exception to this upward and diagonal emphasis was the square and solid central tower, which appeared the work of another architect.

At the end of the top terrace were three steps up to a seat, known as the Quarter-Deck, the highest point of the St Beuno's property. From there a great holly hedge stretched down the hill past beehives and the summer-house, and disappeared into the tree-mass near the Tremeirchion road. Magpies, hawks, crows, flycatchers, finches, woodpigeons and the occasional robin made the only sounds apart from winds in the trees, although further below were animal-noises on the St Beuno's farm, Ty-Mawr (the Big House), opposite the Rock Chapel. And the college donkeys were continually braying in the lower field near the gate; sometimes when donkeys were unavailable students took their place between the shafts to do the hauling. The main feature of the gardens was undoubtedly the centre walk from the long row of firs which bordered the gardens high up on Maenefa, down ten short flights of steps with long descending intervals between, past the baroque urns used as geranium pots, and intermittent pairs of uglily shaped yew bushes, with on either side rows of fruit trees and berry bushes, cabbages, beans and peas, flowers, and herbs; through the flat central small formal garden of grass and gravel, with flower beds, where the old priests, known as the Cur. Vals, who had been sent to St Beuno's to finish their days, walked about; and down to the Broad Walk and lawns and pond among the beeches, chestnuts, ilex, oak and ash, just above the road.

On his first day at St Beuno's Hopkins saw the Crows' Nests, platforms constructed aloft in the sturdiest trees near the Tremeirchion road, and had been introduced to a perennial topic of jokes and complaints, the noisy central-heating system, or, as he called it, 'pipes of affliction' conveying 'lukewarm water of affliction to some of the rooms' (*L3*, 124). During the coldest weather it tended to go on strike, but compensated on warmer days, and the tale was told of how the sub-librarian was found sitting in his room with window open and collar off, gasping for breath. The building of the new extension had at last been completed, so that the previously cramped community could now expand into the new part of the west wing. Their only regret was that there was no increased bathing accommodation; and then the water supply was most unreliable, especially in the summer months when the wells were low. A current topic of conversation was that Penance in the refectory had had to be sacrificed while the new wing was being built, on account of curious workmen peering through the windows.

Henry Kerr, a former Commander in the Royal Navy, who had distinguished himself in the Crimean War, may have been persuaded to give an account of the annual holiday, known as the 'Villa', the previous year at Barmouth, when the Jesuits and the Benedictines of Downside, the two orders of 'Black Monks', underwent extensive naval manoeuvres under the supervision of Kerr, known as 'the Admiral' for the occasion. Father Hogan had been seasick, and was given a mock court-martial aboard the yacht 'Jolly Dog' for being 'found drunk and incapable in the scuppers'. The same 'Jolly Dog' had sailed on the morning of 12 August for Bardsey Island with the Rector on board, who had with him all the requisites for Mass there the next morning. When a stiff breeze blew up that evening some anxiety had been felt, but was allayed when a telegram was received: 'Weatherbound STOP Bardsey to-morrow STOP Home to-morrow evening'. Mr Lund, 'sent forward with despatches', had run seven miles to Pwllheli to send the telegram, anxious to relieve the anxiety of the community and of Lady Ratcliffe, whose husband was with the expedition.

After his first full day at St Beuno's Hopkins had formed a rough idea of the content of the Theologians' course: 'lectures in dogmatic theology, moral ditto, canon law, church history, scripture, Hebrew and what not' (L3, 124); there was still a month before his studies started, at the beginning of October, and a week and a half before his annual eight-day retreat.

September was considered one of the best times for exploring the environs of St Beuno's. The countryside was crossed by direct drovers' roads or sometimes a straighter Roman one, contrasted with the narrowest of winding, ill-surfaced and muddy hilly lanes and by-ways, which secluded many of the smaller villages. It was a land of woods, caves, disused mine-shafts, wells, and many burial tumuli, cairns, sites of battles, the occasional ivy-covered castle ruins, and farms constructed on the picturesque ruins of an ancient Dominican priory or house of Templars or Carmelite Friary. Weeping and wailing airs, such as the 'Morfa Rhuddlan', still kept alive in folk music otherwise forgotten defeats of the native Cymry by the invader tyrant Saxon. There were still many patches left of the woodland across which, it used to be said, a squirrel could travel from the Dee estuary to the west coast without once touching the ground. The only signs in the Vale of Clwyd of the Industrial Revolution were the smoke from the lime-kilns and the chuffing of the occasional steam-engines. These did not obtrude: Hopkins came to see the kiln smoke as a fitting natural feature of the valley.

On his third day in Wales Hopkins walked with Francis Bacon back across the Rhuallt crossroads and by the Smithy Arms on to the Cwm and Dyserth road, winding along the eastern side of the Clwyd hills, or the 'pastoral forehead of Wales' as he saw it ('The Wreck of the Deutschland', st. 24), which hindered the access of the biting east gales, and made the predominant winds the pleasantly moist north-west and sou'wester. The temperature in the vale was never extreme, checked as it was by the sea, although one Rector of the college wrote that 'the cruel east wind in April and May was apt to find its way through clefts in the hills, and make havoc of the vegetation and of human life' (*Hunter*, 43). There were woods and grazing-lands up the slope on their right, beyond the brambles and flourishing hedgerows. Ahead of them were the constant landmarks of the Great Orme headland to the left, and on the right the coastal resort of Rhyl – 'this shallow and frail town', as Hopkins came to call it ('The Sea and the Skylark'). On their left was the wide Vale of Clwyd, some of the most fertile land in North Wales, enriched by the affable climate. Strangers had often found the valley attractive, and Defoe's words in the 1720s still seemed appropriate, as though machines had never been invented:

> That which was most surprising, after such a tiresome and fatiguing journey ... was that descending now from the hills, we came into a most pleasant, fruitful, populous, and delicious vale, full of villages and towns, the fields shining with corn, just ready for the reapers, the meadows green and flowery, and a fine river,

with a mild and gentle stream running through it; nor is it a small or casual intermission, for we had a prospect of the country open before us, for above 20 miles in length, and from 5 to 7 miles in breadth, all smiling with the same kind of complexion.
(*Defoe*, 387-8)

And Defoe added: 'which made us think our selves in England again, all on a sudden', and more recent visitors had compared it with the Oxfordshire countryside. Unlike the wilder north-west and central mountainous areas of the country, which were often considered by tourists to be typically Welsh, the Vale of Clwyd possessed for Hopkins amenable, charming qualities similar to those of his favourite Devonshire and Oxfordshire patches of countryside. Later on, whenever he generalised about Wales, he was always remembering this area within walking distance of St Beuno's.

Hopkins and Bacon came to the tiny hidden hill-village of Cwm, a collection of houses on the sides of a triangle formed by three tracks, two of which led off the Dyserth road up the hillside. It was so called because its centre was a narrow sequestered valley which formed a coomb – a shape which Hopkins had often identified and fondly responded to in the past, on his recent Devonshire holiday and when he had been with his family on the Isle of Wight as an adolescent. But the Clwyd valley had no villages of the kind with which English people would be familiar. A St Beuno's Jesuit wrote:

An English village consists of a number of houses gathered together round a green, and close to the old church rectory and the manor-house, and the rest of the inhabitants of the parish are found in a few large farmhouses. With us there are commonly few houses near the church, and old rectories and manor-houses are things almost unknown. It is not that the population is thin, but they are scattered, and every sheltered nook among the hills will be found to be occupied by a farm-house. There are few cottages, for the farmers seldom have capital enough to be able to employ many labourers, but they employ their own families to work the land.
(*Hunter*, 43)

Cwm was dominated and hidden on the seaward side by Y Foel, the Voel or bare mountain, and to the south-east by Mynydd y Cwm,

Cwm mountain, and Coed Cwm, the wood on its upper slopes and around its summit. Among its cottages was Llew Glas, the Blue Lion Inn, and only six paces away, on the other side of the road, a wall encircled the sloping yard of the parish church dedicated to two local Celtic saints, Mael and Sulien. Notices showed that church services were in the Welsh language here in the long and low barn-like building of rough stone without spire or tower, but with a simple chimney-like bellcote at one end of the roof. Beneath its ancient porch was a wooden door with rows of large nail-heads. The strangest tomb was the elaborate hooded one of Grace Williams. In spite of the familiar English churchyard look of cypress, and names like William, Martha, Margaret, Elizabeth and Henry on tombstones, many carved names were Welsh.

It is likely that Hopkins saw his first Welsh kestrels on this walk, as they were usually more numerous around the ferns below the Cwm road, about a hundred feet below the summit of Y Foel, than they were on Maenefa. On this walk Hopkins passed small farms and dwellings, all with Welsh names, like Cil-y-Coed (Wood's Edge), and some with an unpronounceable one, like Bwthyn (the Cottage), which written down appeared to be all consonants, but which when he had been in Wales a while longer seemed to him when spoken to be all vowels. An occasional well with cows grazing nearby was on the gentler slope below the road. They encountered a few people with hidden dark eyes which jerked awkwardly to the strangers' odd clothes and voices, searching for a hint as to what they were doing there.

The road was usually only seven or eight feet wide, narrower than the college galleries, and if a cart overtook them they had to press into the hedgerows, sometimes twenty feet high, and forming into a dark tunnel. Walkers on that road were always conscious of the mountain up one side, and the fertile vale on the other side down beyond the slope. About two hundred yards from the Rhuallt crossroads Maenefa reasserted itself as the dominant feature. The good-natured gentleness of that road back to St Beuno's seemed typified in summer by the thistle-heads blowing about, and by the butterflies haunting its brambles, such as a brown one with magnificent black wings spotted with lemon; there were numerous butterflies in the district, browns, yellows, whites, blacks, blues, and oranges.

The following day Hopkins and Henry Kerr walked east past the little Rock Chapel crowning a lofty and precipitous wooded hill above the road to Tremeirchion (the homestead of Meirchion). The village church old school was crudely built of rough stone, like a labourer's cottage with a brick entrance-porch added. Next door was the old inn, the low and rambling Salusbury Arms, with several small windows. This was Hopkins's first encounter with the district's many connections with Dr Johnson; the Salusbury family were wealthy and influential landowners, and a John Salusbury had left the huge Flintshire estate of Bach-y-graig to his daughter, Johnson's close companion Mrs. Hester Thrale, who, after a second marriage to an Italian music-teacher, Mr Piozzi, went to live nearby in 1795. Then there was the crude old Corpus Christi church, one of the few Welsh country churches containing an organ, with stone seats by the lych-gate, an Elizabethan font, and a sundial dated 1748, formed from the shaft of a fourteenth-century cross, whose head, with four ogee canopies covering carved figures, had been an object of pilgrimage and especial devotion in Catholic times (and which, a few years after Hopkins's visit, would be sold by the parish to pay for church repairs, and re-erected with a new shaft in the St Beuno's courtyard, where it is today). Inside the church was a wall-tablet informing that Mrs Piozzi was buried in a vault on the north side of the nave. In the beautifully situated circular churchyard, tombstones dated back several hundred years; many were carved in Welsh, with recurring local surnames of Griffiths, Price, Roberts, Edwards, Owen, Morgan, Evans and Morris. Margaret was very common. Again Hopkins puzzled over the strange language precisely craftsman-cut on limestone slabs: 'ER COF AM/ EDWARD WILLIAMS/ CYNT OR TY MAWR/ YR HWN A FU FARW/ MEHEFIN 20. 1865/ YN 64. ML OED./ HEFYD/ LOUIA ei FERCH/ yr hon a gladdwyd/ Mai 28n 1870/ Yn 27 ml oed'.

On the other side of the church was the new school, built eight years before, very neatly, in uneven limestone rectangles, like St Beuno's. Tremeirchion was a hillside village like Cwm, consisting of a handful of rough-stone two-storey houses and labourers' primitive thick white cottages, and flourishing gardens of vegetables, fruit and flowers. The rambling whitewashed buildings of an ancient smithy were settled around three sides of a square, with the road the fourth side. At the junction of the St Beuno's-Rhuallt and St Asaph to Denbigh roads they came across a lodgekeeper's three-bay ashlar cottage, next to the rusticated sandstone gatepiers and elaborate ironwork gates at the start of a long wooded drive which wound round to Brynbella, the neo-classical mansion with a Welsh-Italian name which Mr and Mrs Piozzi had built eighty years before. Hopkins was introduced to the ancient lodge-keeper, and was thrilled to learn from her that, before she entered the employ of Brynbella's present owner Mr Ralli, she had been servant to Mrs Piozzi, Mrs Thrale that was, though she did not remember seeing Dr Johnson. She was a Tremeirchion Cow, she said, and there were Denbigh Cats, Cwm Calves, and Caerwys Crows (*L3*, 125). Hopkins remembered this when he later adopted as his Welsh bardic signature 'Brân Maenefa', the Crow of Maenefa, to disguise the authorship of two poems he wrote, although, as at that time he was the only Jesuit at St Beuno's who could speak Welsh, it would be plain to everyone there that they were his.

The walls of Brynbella's grounds stretched for some way down by the side of the steep road continuing through Tremeirchion village. At the estate's southernmost point the road met the Trefnant and Denbigh road, and opposite this junction was the Ffynnon Beuno Inn, behind a triangular ground where carriages could pull off the main road. By the side of the inn was a separate brick and stone building with a large hand-pump attached to its outside wall, and on an adjacent wall water gushed from the distortedly large mouth of a worn grotesque stone head. Within these walls was a disused square brick-lined large bath, Ffynnon Faenol or Ffynnon Beuno (St Beuno's Well), with steps leading down into it at one corner. In the inn were kept the keys for the well. In the hill behind were the mouths of two prehistoric limestone caves which, after excavation in the 1880s, would reveal pre-ice-age mammoth, hyena, rhinoceros, and human remains. Underneath the steep Graig Tremeirchion beyond the inn was St Beuno Cottage, and below the narrow lane were the tall chimneys and steep gables of the prosperous and beautiful cramped Jacobean buildings and cruder rambling outhouses of

Henblas Farm. Beyond the farm straggling farmhouses and cottages formed the southern limits of the village.

Some hedges of these narrow lanes were bramble, with flowers and blackberries showing, but it was more common to see aged hedges with masses of many kinds of vegetation in jumbled profusion, hawthorn, ivy, holly, grasses and a wide variety of wild flowers. After that walk Hopkins noted in his journal: 'A silvery-brown blindworm was gliding over the road.– Hardhead, crosswort, agrimony (J, 257).

The next day he and a companion walked to the straggling village-city of St Asaph, an English name which had been unknown before 1100. The people still called it by its older, Welsh name of Llan-elwy, 'the place of the church on the Elwy', the river from whose banks it stretched across to the river Clwyd. The two men passed another of Mrs Hemans's houses, Bronwylfa, surrounded by pleasure grounds and a thickly wooded park, near the station, and saw her monument in the cathedral. Her sweet and holy poetic productions were said to be the reflex of her personal and mental beauties ('there was a dove-like look in her eyes, a chastened sadness in her expression'). Mrs Hemans was reputed to have said that her heart beat too loudly, even in the quiet Vale of Clwyd, and she had passed away, 'almost etherealised'. Like Hopkins she had some red hair and lived only until her early forties, before dying, like him, in Dublin.

Visiting St Asaph, the smallest of all English and Welsh cathedrals, in 1774, Dr Johnson had written that 'though not large, [it] has something of dignity and grandeur', and Hopkins's first impression was similar: 'Though it is no bigger than a large parish church it has an imposing rather cathedral-like look. It has old choir-stalls and a massive tower' (J, 257). This conspicuous embattled tower, dating from 1392, was ninety-three feet high, and from its top there was an extensive view of the Vale of Clwyd. The cathedral had been burnt to the ground by Owain Glyndwr in 1402, and in Cromwell's time horses had been stabled in the choir-stalls. The modern predators were the gothic architectural restorers. Hopkins wrote that it was 'restoring and restored, with the usual consequence that its historical interest is gone and you cannot tell what is old, what new' (L3, 126). At the time of his visit it was in the hands of the archetypal over-prolific restorer Sir Gilbert Scott, and would not be re-opened until a year later, when the nave and aisles were completed. Many of the restorations there were afterwards considered conjectural and unsatisfactory, though the 1986 Buildings of Wales volume judged that Scott 'gave back an E[arly] E[nglish] appearance to the N and S sides, authentic in the elements, if not completely so in detail', and his fittings were 'thoroughly good'.

Two days later, however, Hopkins expressed in his journal his admiration for the Holy Trinity memorial church at the village of Trefnant, in the Decorated style, which, though he did not realise it, had been built to Scott's designs in 1855. Hopkins wrote that he liked 'the pretty little new church built of the same limestone as St Beuno's and the pillars of a mottled grey, I suppose local, marble. Capitals all of that sort which is common – two rows or rings of tufts of leaf or flower, one above the other, the upper the bigger, and the two rows alternate with one another. These were good work' (J, 257). These Ruskinian stonecarvings, grouped in threes to symbolise the Holy Trinity, had been copied under Scott's direction by a Denbigh craftsman J. Blinstone, from wild flowers and leaves he had gathered from local hedges and woods. Hopkins also admired the corbels, straightforwardly realistic carvings of men's and women's heads. The church was delicately and quietly decorated, with a simple lack of shouting rhetoric, and so quite an alien contrast to the churches of Hopkins's usual favourite architect, William Butterfield.

At the start of their walk to Trefnant Hopkins and Purbrick had made their way through the St Beuno's gardens and fields to the Rock, a large limestone landmark, purchased in 1859, which dominated the valley; on its summit was the tiny Rock Chapel, dedicated to Our Lady of Sorrows, and built by a corps of volunteer Irish navvies in their spare time from constructing the local railway line. Designed by a St Beuno's student who had been an architect, it was intended 'to make reparation to our Lady for the sanctuaries that had been snatched from her in the Vale of Clwyd'. It could be seen distinctly for miles from the broad valley below, and in the distance it strangely produced all the effects of a much larger and statelier church. The community had nevertheless seldom been able to find a practical use for the chapel, and it was kept locked; Hopkins did not mention it in letters, only the hawks and owls flying in and out of the trees below it.

After a seven-mile walk the following Sunday, and a fairly arduous climb through heath and furze, Hopkins and William Kerr reached the summit of Moel-y-Parc and looked down the valley to Rhyl, where the Clwyd joined the sea, and south up the valley to the quaint little hill-town of Ruthin. Below lay the villages of Caerwys and Bodfari, in the cleave made by the Afon Chwiler, the river Wheeler. That evening Hopkins described what he had seen:

> It was a leaden sky, braided or roped with cloud, and the earth in dead colours, grave but distinct. The heights by Snowdon were hidden by the clouds but not from distance or dimness. The nearer hills, the other side of the valley, shewed a hard and beautifully detached and glimmering brim against the light, which was lifting there. All the length of the valley the skyline of hills was flowingly written all along upon the sky. A blue bloom, a sort of meal, seemed to have spread upon the distant south, enclosed by a basin of hills. Looking all round but most in looking far up the valley I felt an instress and charm of Wales.
> (J, 258)

Soon before their theology course was due to begin Hopkins and Francis Bacon walked to the second, more beautiful river valley, that of the Elwy. From the height of the Cefn Rocks, near the cave where the earliest evidence of human occupation of Wales had been found a year or two before, Hopkins saw:

> the view of the deep valley of the Elwy, the meeting of two, which makes three, glens indeed, is most beautiful. The woods, thick and silvered by sunlight and shade, by the flat smooth banking of the tree-tops expressing the slope of the hill, came down to the green bed of the valley. Below at a little timber bridge I looked at some delicate flying shafted ashes – there was one especially of single sonnet-like inscape – between which the sun sent straight bright slenderish panes of silvery sunbeams down the slant towards the eye and standing above an unkept field stagged with patchy yellow heads of ragwort.
> (J, 259)

One night Hopkins climbed the narrow ladder through a trap-door on to the roof of the four-storey college tower, and from that vantage-point watched a fine sunset. 'The place is famous for them', he wrote in his journal (J, 259), and a note of cynicism can be detected. Expected responses were not his strong point, and although the sunset had been a fine one he did not write it up.

Just before the scholastic year started Hopkins strolled in the beautiful woods near the village of Caerwys, once a Roman station, and with Joseph Rickaby, a student on the same course, climbed Maenefa, noticing when they reached the summit that the multi-hued smokes issuing from kilns in the valley did not spoil the beautiful liquid-blue wash which covered all the landscape. Another evening he again watched the sun set, and this time felt unpressured and able to write about it, using private language which shows his comparative lack of interest in communication:

> a lovely sunset of rosy juices and creams and combs; the combs I mean scattered floating bats or rafts or racks above, the creams/ the strew and bed of the sunset, passing north and south or rather north only into grey marestail and brush along the horizon to the hills. Afterwards the rosy field of the sundown turned gold and the slips and creamings in it stood out like brands, with jots of purple. A sodden twilight over the valley and foreground all below, holding the corner-hung maroon-grey diamonds of ploughfields to one keeping but allowing a certain glare in the green of the tufts of grass.
> (J, 260)

Three
'So lavish and so beautiful': Wells

September 10th, 1874, when Hopkins had been in Wales almost a fortnight, was a fine and bright day, and moreover a special holiday, known to Jesuits as a Blandyke. So he and Bacon walked to another of the district's sights, Ffynnon Fair, well-known as a tourist beauty spot. Down the road to Tremeirchion, then branching right on to the pretty lane to Trefnant, past the cut corn-fields until after two miles they came to a humped-back bridge over the river Clwyd, where the narrow and shallow stream gave excellent fishing. At Trefnant they followed the St Asaph road until they had crossed Pont-yr-allt, a bridge over the Elwy. At the Pont-yr-allt mill, they turned on to a cart-way alongside the bank of the narrow meandering river, with a soft and wet green tree-lined meadow on their right. In the distance was a clump of trees, and making for this they crossed a little mill-race by a bridge. The clump was guarded by railings for the most part, and was shaded by overspreading elm and sycamore on a muddy hill. In its centre they saw Ffynnon Fair or Ffynnon-y-capel, Mary's Well or the Chapel Well. This was one of close on a hundred in Wales dedicated to Mary, who had seemed so alive to the medieval Welsh that it was often said that she had visited the country. There were known to be six Ffynhonnau Fair in Denbighshire alone, besides numerous Lady wells, Our Lady wells, and Mary wells. She had been by far the most popular of the non-Celtic saints with wells dedicated to them in Wales. (Francis Jones, *The Holy Wells of Wales* [Cardiff, 1954])

Ffynnon Fair consisted of a well and a ruined chapel, some of whose stone walls contained remnants of third-pointed gothic

41

windows and doorways, though it lacked a roof and its floor was a tangle of weeds. The well formed the western arm of the cruciform chapel, with a baptismal trough, no longer evident, once forming the essential connection between chapel and well. Hopkins's drawing of the well in his journal was done after his visit from memory, and has several inaccuracies. From the fissured limestone bottom of the well the cold and pure spring water gushed up, forcefully breaking the surface, then splaying outwards to the five points of the well-surround; from there it flowed into a large bath, and out into a stream which encircled part of the chapel. The five points recalled the five porticoes of 'the house of mercy', Bethesda, in the third chapter of St John's gospel, under which crowds of sick people gathered to be healed by the waters. Stumps of pillars were all that remained of a stone canopy over the well, after its desecration in the sixteenth century, when the visible and outward signs of the Roman Catholic faith had been removed from Britain by the reformers.

The holy well and ruined chapel in its beautiful river-meadow setting were to tourists a romantic aid in delicious imaginative attempts to re-create a medieval past which in their sentimentality they pictured as more interesting than their own uninspiring times. But Catholics would experience a particular poignancy about this once famous place, one of the district's many examples of holy ruins no longer treated with devotion by worshipping man. The Catholic history of Britain would be reawakened for them, and in a most vivid way they could imagine the dreadful time of the Reformation, when 'effigies were removed, church wall-paintings obliterated, rood-lofts and shrines destroyed, pilgrimages to wells and sacred sites prohibited', and above all when the continuous and living sacred line of the Church in Britain had been suddenly broken off.

On returning to St Beuno's Hopkins wrote in his journal: 'we said a prayer and drank the water' (J, 258). In so doing he was continuing a traditional practice of well-worship that went back to pre-Christian times. In the earliest literature wells had been associated with gods, oracles, sacrifices, festivals, burials, megaliths, and trees. The life of the medieval Welsh had been 'intensely concerned with wells and well-chapels', the sister wells of Ffynnon Fair, Holywell, and Cwm (which Hopkins did not know about) attracting widespread veneration, pilgrimages being made throughout the year. Some, such as that of St Winefride at Holywell, were particularly elaborate, and were associated with miraculous cures. Fourteenth- and fifteenth-century bards like Iolo Goch, Brydydd Hir, and Tudur Aled had sung the praises of Winefride and the cures at her well. Then under Henry VIII Wales became legally part of the realm of England, and the four Welsh dioceses part of an autonomous Church of England, of which the king was 'supreme head'. All the great religious houses and the lesser monasteries in Wales were suppressed in 1536, and wells, relics and pilgrimages denounced as superstition.

The Reformation had not encountered much opposition among the leading clergy and the great landowning families of Wales, but there was some Catholic opposition from the sixteenth-century bards, such as Thomas ap Ifan ap Rhys, and Sion Brwynog of Anglesey, who, in his *Cywydd y Ddwy Ffydd* (*Cywydd* to the Two Faiths), powerfully combined poetry and racialism in scornfully denouncing the new-fangled religion and the manners of its exponents. For a hundred years or so Welsh poems written down by hand circulated around the villages praising and lamenting over the Mass, our Lady, the Welsh saints, rosaries and roods, monasteries, shrines and wells. But the ordinary people remained bewildered after the shrines were destroyed, their sites prohibited, and holy effigies which had presided over lonely wells had been removed and defaced or burnt. And they remained largely apathetic towards any form of religion until Welsh Nonconformity provided a spiritual leadership which had been lacking since the Middle Ages.

But the well cult, which in one form or another had existed before Christianity, had a darker and deeper hold on people's minds and needs, despite the sneers of the educated at such quaint survivals and gross superstitions. Tales circulated about the various forms of potency wells possessed. St Winefride's Well and Chapel had never been destroyed, and pilgrimages with resulting cures continued there, although forbidden by law and, according to the new teaching, contrary to the good of men's souls. And although the Ffynnon Fair chapel by the Elwy had been laid waste, clandestine marriages continued to be celebrated there as late as 1640, its remoteness making it suitable for Gretna Green tactics. In 1810 Meyrick, a Protestant, wrote: 'The lower order of people ... are uncommonly superstitious, nor has the light of reformation overcome those bigotted prejudices originally received from the Druids, and afterwards with equal zeal cherished by the Roman Catholics'. In the 1850s a woman begged George Borrow to 'stay and taste the *dwr santaidd* of the holy well':

> 'What holy well is that?' said I.
> 'A well,' said she, 'by the road's side, which in the time of the popes was said to perform wonderful cures.'
> 'Let us taste it by all means,' said I; whereupon she went out, and presently returned with a tray on which were a jug and tumbler, the jug filled with the water of the holy well; we drank some of the *dwr santaidd* which tasted like any other water.
> (*Borrow*, 74)

Except in the solitary instance of St Winefride's Well, the Reformation had succeeded in suppressing official Catholic wellrites; but quite apart from surreptitious or arcane religious patronage, the hold of the wells over people's minds continued into the eighteenth and nineteenth centuries, manifesting itself more and more in new secular romantic forms. Protestant travellers like Celia Fiennes in 1698, Defoe in the 1720s, and Dr Johnson in 1774, had been cynical but fascinated by St Winefride's Well, while since the early seventeenth century, and increasingly in the eighteenth and nineteenth, artists such as Thomas Dinely, Francis Place and the Bucks had sketched and painted the more picturesque wells. And the poetic tradition relating to wells had been unbroken since the medieval Welsh bards, although its character had undergone many changes. In 1823 an anonymous writer published a poem in Welsh on the Marvels of Wales, which described St Winefride's and the ebb and flow well near Rhuddlan, five miles from St Beuno's.

Then with the increasing desire of English tourists to visit sublime Welsh scenery came several poems on wells written by English people. Mrs Hemans wrote 'Our Lady's Well' on this same Ffynnon Fair, and Hopkins probably knew 'East and West', published in Matthew Arnold's *New Poems* of 1867. Arnold had taken a holiday in North Wales in August 1864, during which he had written to his sister that 'the poetry of the Celtic race and its names of places quite overpowers me'. The poem gives Arnold's version of the legend concerning Ffynnon Seiriol and Ffynnon Gybi, two springs, ten yards apart, at Clorach in the middle of Anglesey. Some wells had featured in novels, such as St John's Well, Glamorgan, in R.D. Blackmore's *Maid of Sker*.

Holy wells were a peculiarly Welsh feature, and whether, like Ffynnon Fair, disused and merely a picturesque ruin, or, like St Winefride's, in continuous use from the Middle Ages to the present day, they were of overridingly poignant historical interest to an earnest mid-Victorian professional Catholic, particularly one whose feelings and thoughts were as involved with poetry as Hopkins's.

*   *   *

On 8 October Hopkins saw St Winefride's Well for the first time:

> Bright and beautiful day. Crests of snow could be seen on the mountains. Barraud and I walked over to Holywell and bathed at the well and returned very joyously. The sight of the water in the well as clear as glass, greenish like beryl or aquamarine, trembling at the surface with the force of the springs, and shaping out the five foils of the well quite drew and held my eyes to it. Within a month or six weeks from this (I think Fr. di Pietro said) a young man from Liverpool, Arthur Kent (?), was cured of rupture/ in the water. The strong unfailing flow of the water and the chain of cures from year to year all these centuries took hold of my mind with wonder at the bounty of God in one of His saints, the sensible thing so naturally and gracefully uttering the spiritual reason of its being (which is all in true keeping with the story of St Winefride's death and recovery) and the spring in place leading back the thoughts by its spring in time to its spring in eternity: even now the stress and buoyancy and abundance of the water is before my eyes.
>
> (*J*, 261)

He had known and thought about this well for a long time before he first encountered its reality. In September 1867, when he was already a Roman Catholic but before he entered the Jesuit novitiate, Hopkins was on holiday at Bovey Tracey in Devon, staying with his Oxford friend the Revd E.W. Urquhart, and one morning he walked to Newton Abbott for Mass, which was said by a mission-priest Kenelm Vaughan, one of the famous Catholic family, some of whom Hopkins had previously met. Afterwards Hopkins had breakfast with the priest, and spent most of that day at St Augustine's Priory, Abbotsleigh, with Vaughan, who 'impressed many, including his brother the Cardinal, as a man of remarkable asceticism and saintliness'. Vaughan told Hopkins that he had once been

> in consumption, dying: the sisters had a novena for him and he was drinking water from St Winefred's well: one Sunday he had crept down to say Mass, when, there being no rain, before the consecration a quantity of water fell on him and the altar so that he sent to ask the Canon whether he should consecrate or not: he was told to do so and Mass went on: after Mass he was perfectly well. He had two enthusiasms – for the B. Sacrament and for the bible. He has a silver lamp to burn before the bible in his room to make reparation to God for the desecrated use that has been made of it for these 300 years.
> (J, 157)

It is probable that Hopkins decided that day on his vocation, and that subsequently St Winefride and her well held a deep fascination for him.

* * *

St Winefride's story had first been recorded several hundred years after her death, by twelfth-century monks. Winefride, or, to call her by her true, Welsh, name, Gwenfrewi, was the daughter of a chieftain Tewyth ap Eylud and his wife Gwenlo, who probably lived at Bryn-y-Castell in the province of Tegeingl, in modern Flintshire. Caradoc, a chieftain from Penarlag, English Hawarden, attempted to seduce her one Sunday while her parents were at Mass; she ran towards the church built by her uncle Beuno, but Caradoc caught and beheaded her. At the previously dry place where her head fell a spring started up. Beuno replaced the head on the body, whereupon Winefride regained life and lived another fifteen years as a nun, with a white scar encircling her neck. Beuno cursed Caradoc, who was swallowed up by the earth.

There was nothing unique about Winefride's tale, an assortment of details from Celtic legend piously arranged. The pattern of Winefride's martyrdom was frequently found, as was the emergence of wells and replacement of severed heads. St Llud had also been beheaded by a pursuer, on Slwch Hill, Brecknockshire, and 'her head rowling a little down the hill, a Cleare Spring of Water Issued out of the Rock where it rested'. Hopkins advised Bridges to look up the story in Butler's *Lives*, but added 'though you should treat it as a fable, as no doubt you do the Gospels' (L1, 40). The story is probably a Christianised version of a common northern pagan legend in which the pursuer succeeds in deflowering the maiden before killing her, and a spring gushes forth on the spot to signify the natural restoration of her maidenhead, rather than her actual head (see for example Ingmar Bergman's film *The Virgin Spring*).

St Winefride's cult was at first associated with that of St Beuno, and like his was for a few hundred years confined to North Wales. Her well became the most prominent of a number of North Welsh centres of pilgrimage, which included Rhuddlan, Yr Wyddrug, and Tremeirchion (at all of which there were famous roods), and the wells of St Dyfnog at Llanrhaedr-yng-Nghinmeirch, and Ffynnon Fair in the parish of Cefn, the stellar shape of which, as Hopkins noted, was similar to that of St Winefride's. There was probably a wooden chapel on the St Winefride's site in the seventh century, which was first replaced by a finer church of stone, and, when this was falling down in the fifteenth century, by the present well-chapel, a fine example of perpendicular architecture. The spring water was artificially directed so that the main gush came up from the earth through static water around it, and emerged on the surface in a ragged shape, which was then captured and directed by the surrounding stone structure into a defined five-pointed star, representing the porches of the Bethesda pool, in which a cure for any ailment, physical or mental, might be sought. From this basic structure splendidly proportioned arches rose to form a well-chamber, which acted as crypt and an integral part of the structure of the tiny chapel above.

Pilgrimages were commonplace throughout Europe in the fourteenth and fifteenth centuries, by which time St Winefride's Well was famous all over Britain, signposted from as far away as the holy well of Jesmond Dene in Northumberland and from Walsingham in Norfolk, with which shrines it formed a vast triangle of popular pilgrimage. Henry V had prayed to Winefride before his victory at Agincourt and made a pilgrimage of thanks on foot to the well in 1416; this probably caused Winefride's feast to be raised to major status. Other kings, such as Richard III, were associated with the well, and Winefride was one of the saints whose effigies the first Welsh king of England, Henry VII, chose to watch perpetually over the tomb in his chapel at Westminster. Henry VII's mother, Lady Margaret Countess of Richmond, was one of the chief benefactors behind the building of the new well-chapel, which was supervised by the Abbot of Basingwerk, Thomas Pennant.

Nicholas Pennant, son of Thomas, was Abbot of Basingwerk and guardian of the well at the dissolution of the monastery in 1537. The offerings at Holywell by this time were so valuable that the chapel escaped the otherwise general desecration by Henry VIII and Thomas Cromwell, and was leased to William Holcroft, who collected the chapel offerings and sent them to the king. During Mary's brief reign the chapel was returned to the care of a priest. In Elizabeth's time, as the rich abbey of the Cistercian monks of Basingwerk, who had cared for the well and chapel for three hundred years, had been destroyed, the hounded and itinerant Society of Jesus were secretly charged with its care. The well became an important centre of Catholic resistance to the Church of England, although, surprisingly, persecution of Catholics there was sporadic and half-hearted.

The first and one of the most remarkable of the Jesuit fathers in charge of the Holywell mission had been John Bennet, who was trained at Douai and arrived at Holywell in 1574. He was caught, condemned to death in the chapel in 1582, but imprisoned instead and banished. Returning to Holywell five years later he adopted various aliases, like most Elizabethan Jesuits, of Price, Lloyd and Baker. Although several Jesuits connected with the well were pursued, imprisoned or executed, pilgrimages to the shrine grew in number, and the chapel was still undamaged, while the Jesuits recorded cures at the well. The Star Inn was bought as a hospice for pilgrims and became the official Holywell residence of the Jesuits.

James II and his queen Mary of Modena travelled to Holywell to pray for a son, and 'when the Prince of Wales was born it was thought St Winefride's prayers had done it'. During the Protestant reaction against the threat of a Catholic heir, a crowd plundered the Star Inn.

But pilgrimages continued during the eighteenth century, despite persecution; even as late as 1715 a Jesuit, Philip Leigh, is reported as having to adopt the aliases of Layton and Metcalfe. In 1724 however, Defoe's account of Holywell suggests that public authorities used to turn a blind eye to the goings-on at the well:

> [Holywell] may indeed be said to have arisen from the confluence of the people hither, for almost all the houses are either public houses, or let into lodgings; and the priests that attend here, and are very numerous, appear in disguise. Sometimes they are physicians, sometimes surgeons, sometimes gentlemen, and sometimes patients or any thing as occasion presents. No body takes notice of them as to their profession, though they know them well enough, no not the Roman Catholics themselves; but in private they have their proper oratories in certain places whither their votaries resort; and good manners have prevailed so far, that however the Protestants know who and who's together, no body takes notice of it, or enquires where one another goes, or has been gone.
> (Defoe, 388-9)

Early in the nineteenth century the chapel at the old Star Inn was licensed for public use, and with an increasing number of pilgrims to the well, it became again, openly, the major interest of the town of Holywell. In the decade before Hopkins visited the well, a convent and a hospice were established to provide hospitality and aid to pilgrims, and more recently the Jesuits of the Holywell mission had further improved the well's facilities. In 1873 the priest in charge whom Hopkins met, Fr John Baptist di Pietro, obtained a lease on the well from its owners the Holywell Town Council, at £162 per annum. By the time of Hopkins's visit all the area surrounding the outer bath had been fitted with wooden cubicles for bathers to change in, and large screens had been erected to prevent passers-by on the road from looking in (in 1774 Dr Johnson had complained 'the bath is completely and indecently open: a woman bathed while we all looked on'). There were now fixed bathing-times for men of 6 to 8 a.m. and noon to 3 p.m., and ladies from 8 to noon and 3 to 6 p.m.

The well's cures had been continuous from medieval times to the present. The private Jesuit publication *Letters and Notices* for 1872 carried two testimonials of 'wonderful cures' wrought at St Winefride's Well. One was of Thomas Arthur, Viscount Southwell, who was cured on Wednesday 19 July 1871 of 'indigestion, great debility, and low spirits': 'I bathed every morning in the Well here, and when absent always took the moss and water every day'. And Julia Hammond, who had been 'low and weak ever since her con-finement in October, 1867', was cured on Saturday 7 October 1871. Both testimonies were dated within a fortnight of the cure, have vaguely expressed ailments, and are none too convincing, but other cures were undoubtedly genuine. Some time between October 1874 and April 1875 Hopkins tried to follow up at least one supposed cure, of Arthur Kent from Liverpool, and he promised to send the result of his enquiries to his father. He received no confirmation, though he had 'heard of another cure having just been worked in London by the moss or water and am going to enquire into that' (*L3*, 132). But as with many projects announced in his letters home to Hampstead, Hopkins makes no further reference to this. On the slimy walls around the well, however, hung numerous cripples' aids, left there as tokens by grateful pilgrims. And the pillars and walls around the well bore fascinating witness to its history, in carved pictorial symbols, monograms, and names and initials of benefactors, restorers, and the grateful. A stone let into the side of the well bore the Jesuit monogram IHS and the date 1687, the year when James II and his queen had made the pilgrimage. An elaborate Chi Rho, for Christ, was next to the date 1627, and nearer Hopkins's time there were several Irish names, such as 'James Cuff. Sligo. July. 1849 cured he[re]'. But also, in a graveyard above the chapel, were engraved the names of pilgrims to Holywell who had died there uncured.

The well came to mean more to Hopkins than any other single natural object in Wales. It appeared to combine ultimate religious values with a powerfully emotive natural feature in an incredibly unified all-round symbolism. It represented God showing himself to man through nature in so positive and straightforward and yet poetic a way that Hopkins must have felt all his religious strivings and all his poetic, literary strivings had come together at last. It combined so many features in such a whole, simple way. One part of the well's symbolism was that it was the only shrine in the British Isles with a continuous history of Catholic pilgrimage. Pious visits to this shrine had never died out; so it was a means of keeping the true faith within Britain, a token offered to God that in this one locality at least Hopkins's native land had remained true and faithful. The fact that the Society of Jesus had kept the shrine and the faith alive must have been to Hopkins an encouraging sign of justification in his vocation. The continuous record of cures suggested that in the one small area that post-Reformation British man had preserved for the true faith, God repaid his servants in a symbolic mutual give-and-take relationship, showing 'the bounty of God', as Hopkins wrote. Then there were the various pieces of symbolism woven together in Winefride's story. The martyrdom for the principle of her virginity must have seemed justification of professional chastity, 'a eunuch for the kingdom of heaven's sake', as Hopkins less attractively described his own case some years later. Whatever the exact truth was of the original happenings – Winefride's life, death, resurrection, and the well's origin – the story's significance lay in the marvellous continuing bounty of God that the saint's virginity had provoked.

It was a God-given medieval occurrence still happening in godless times, as a beckoning-back symbol. The main symbolism to which Hopkins responded, however, was 'the sensible thing so naturally and gracefully uttering the spiritual reason of its being' (J, 261). All the properties of the well which could be perceived through the senses were not just aesthetically pleasing, but were symbolically perfect, uttering 'the spiritual reason of its being', since it was a natural inscape of God's purpose, quite abnormally direct, so that man easily felt the instress. This was the continuingly powerful benevolent flow of God. And for once man's manufactured architecture was utterly sensitive to God's greater purpose. The water did not escape at random, but was contained and sustained by the stones sensitively placed by dutiful medieval Catholic men in the five pointed recesses. God the divine architect and man the fallible imitator of God's architecture in his attempts at stone analogies, were for this once united in purpose by the natural feature, expressing God's purpose in a peculiarly direct way. No wonder Hopkins felt overjoyed, after all his striving in two distinct ways, the spiritual life and the artistic one, which although loved by him he believed to be on a different, lower plane, unless he could show God's purpose through it, unless he could make it a missionary aid. The accounts of nature in his journal had not mentioned God; the only ulterior purpose he had found in nature up till then had been the half-way, consolidating force of inscape, whose connection with God he had not yet finally made, although he now knew that Duns Scotus would be the key figure. Meanwhile, here in Winefride's Well was the perfect analogy between nature and God, the analogy which all the poems which he was to write at St Beuno's strove for, and yet which he found so difficult to achieve.

With this perfect analogy discovered it was not surprising that Hopkins felt a strong need to put into verse his complex reactions to the well. His English poem of three simple couplets, 'On St Winefred', describes three qualities of the well, and was probably written just before and placed as offering at the statue's foot on St Winefride's day, 3 November 1874:

> *On St Winefred*
> *besides her miraculous cures*
> *filling a bath and turning a mill*
>
> As wishing all about us sweet,
> She brims her bath in cold or heat;
> She lends, in aid of work and will,
> Her hand from heaven to turn a mill –
> Sweet soul! not scorning honest sweat
> And favouring virgin freshness yet.

The poet wonders at the temperature of the well remaining constant, unaffected by the season and so suggesting permanent values beyond those merely regulated by time. Besides issuing in the holy well, the water from the spring provided the power for several mills in Holywell, and had many industrial uses, driving a woollen mill, grinding corn, and making snuff, besides being used in the making of ale, soap, and paper, the trademarks for all of which included an image of the saint. Hopkins praises the saint for not considering such plebeian purposes beneath her. But the lack of life in the poem was due to its being a free translation of a Latin poem, 'In S. Winefridam', probably written by Hopkins for the same occasion. The Latin language itself seemed to provide an additional sanction for writing a poem, Jesuit scholastics traditionally being encouraged to keep their hand in at manipulating what was still for them the international language, and the means of communicating with foreign provinces of the Society. Hopkins also wrote some unfinished Latin elegiacs expressing similar thoughts on the well to those of his journal description, and elaborating the numerological symbolism of the three springs which issued into the well and the five foils enclosing the water.

Hopkins kept the well in mind for the rest of his life, but did not begin his blank-verse tragedy on St Winefride until October 1879, when he was on the temporary staff of St Joseph's, Bedford Leigh, in dark industrial Lancashire, having left Wales two years previously. He spent Christmas 1879 at St Beuno's, bathing in the well which, Hopkins recorded, 'as it is always at the same temperature, was lukewarm and smoked in the frosty air' (L3, 154). But he had no gifts for dramatising human interplay and speech, as he came to realise, and his interest in the play became more sporadic, until it became extinguished by the awful discouragement of everyday life in 1880s Dublin.

Four
'The Welsh landscape has a great charm': The Year at Saint Beuno's

Hopkins arrived at St Beuno's College on Friday 28 August 1874, to join a community of between fifty and sixty, including eight or nine lay brothers, among them a tailor, a carpenter, and a cook.

> The house stands on a steep hillside, it commands the long-drawn valley of the Clwyd to the sea, a vast prospect, and opposite is Snowdon and its range, just now it being bright visible but coming and going with the weather. The air seems to me very fresh and wholesome.... The garden is all heights, terraces, Excelsiors, misty mountain tops, seats up trees called Crows' Nests, flights of steps seemingly up to heaven lined with burning aspiration upon aspiration of scarlet geraniums: it is very pretty and airy but it gives you the impression that if you took a step farther you would find yourself somewhere on Plenlimmon, Conway Castle, or Salisbury Craig.
> (Hopkins to his father, 29 August 1874)

St Beuno's was a self-sufficient community in most respects. Its own farm, Ty-Mawr, was managed by a bailiff, and parts of the college grounds were given over to the cultivation of vegetables and fruit. Sometimes, when the supply of potatoes, meat, or butter was exhausted, they were forced to buy outside. Tremeirchion had no shops, and probably no tradesmen called at the college.

> A silvery-brown blindworm was gliding over the road. – Hardhead, crosswort, agrimony.
> (Journal, 31 August 1874)

The nearest towns were St Asaph and Denbigh, but the college records show that, rather than sending lay brothers there to buy anything not obtainable locally, the minister, Fr Murphy, would usually either order from tradesmen among the Roman Catholic population of Holywell (quite a distance further away), or else order supplies by post from Liverpool or Manchester, from where they would be dispatched by rail. On one occasion the minister ordered a sheep and a side of beef from Manchester because the local price per pound was eightpence halfpenny, while the Manchester price was only sevenpence. Larger purchases, such as timber, bedding, and on one occasion a cloth (bought wholesale for £4. 15s. 0d.) to recover the billiards table, would necessitate a trip to Manchester or Liverpool by the minister, sometimes accompanied by a lay brother. Old mattresses were sent for renovation to Holywell, and the same town provided a craftsman who made two dozen Windsor chairs at 3s. 9d. each.

> Landscape plotted and pieced – fold, fallow, and plough.
> ('Pied Beauty')

In the 1870s the countryside around St Beuno's was divided into much smaller fields than now; the changes started with the world wars and the resulting emphasis on the most economical use of land. There was no modern stockade fencing. Hedges were the most efficient form of boundary: there were many more and thicker hedgerows than nowadays, and dry stonewalling, both of which would have given shelter to animals and required relatively little upkeep. Laying hedges then was not the skilled work it is today, but was done instinctively and well; equally stonewalling was not the 'art' it is today, but a matter-of-fact duty for maintaining the countryside – suitable stones were eagerly purloined from ruined buildings, including churches.

> With Wm. Kerr, who took me up a hill behind ours (ours is Mynefyr), a furze-grown and heathy hill, from which I could look round the whole country, up the valley towards Ruthin and down to the sea. The cleave in which Bodfari and Caerwys lie was close below. It was a leaden sky, braided or roped with cloud, and the earth in dead colours, grave but distinct.
> (Hopkins's journal, 6 September 1874)

Hedges were full of hips and haws, wild gooseberry and strawberry, hazelnuts and acorns; hazelnuts were cracked and eaten, while acorn-cups were used by children as dolls' teacups.

> The dark-out Lucifer ...
> Self-trellises the touch-tree in live green twines
> And loops the fruity boughs with beauty-bines.
> (verse-fragment composed by Hopkins at St Beuno's)

In those cart-and-horse days it didn't matter if there were a hindrance in the middle of fields. There were more groups of trees in the 1870s than now, and it was the norm to see small copses of wild cherry, rowan, damson, and the all-pervading blackberry bushes.

> Wind-beat whitebeam! airy abeles set on a flare!
> ('The Starlight Night')

> The heights by Snowdon were hidden by the clouds but not from distance or dimness. The nearer hills, the other side of the valley, shewed a hard and beautifully detached and glimmering brim against the light, which was lifting there. All the length of the valley the skyline of hills was flowingly written all along upon the sky. A blue bloom, a sort of meal, seemed to have spread upon the distant south, enclosed by a basin of hills. Looking all round but most in looking far up the valley I felt an instress and charm of Wales.
> (Hopkins's journal, 6 September 1874)

There were no pesticides, and so every field would have its own arrays of lots of wild flowers, profusions of many kinds. Fields were often full of red poppies.

> Cefn Rocks, from which the view of the deep valley of the Elwy, the meeting of two, which makes three, glens indeed, is most beautiful. The woods, thick and silvered by sunlight and shade, by the flat smooth banking of the tree-tops expressing the slope of the hill, came down to the green bed of the valley. Below at a little timber bridge I looked at some delicate flying shafted ashes – there was one especially of single sonnet-like inscape – between which the sun sent straight bright slenderish panes of silvery sunbeams down the slant towards the eye and standing above an unkept field stagged with patchy yellow heads of

ragwort. In the evening I watched a fine sunset from the tower: the place is famous for them.
(Hopkins's journal, 10 September 1874)

The local population of about six or seven hundred was predominantly strict Nonconformist, divided among the Calvinistic Methodists, believing strongly in doom and gloom, the Wesleyan Methodists, Baptists, and Congregationalists; but there were also Church of England and Roman Catholics. They were demanding branches of religion, and you had to show your support for your chapel or church, though the different beliefs usually got on well together. The big estates often had their own chapels; servants would go twice on Sundays to services, which would be taken by the landowner or a circuit minister.

I have got a yearning for the Welsh people and would find it in my heart to work for their conversion. However on consideration it seems best to turn my thoughts elsewhere.
(Hopkins to his mother, 20 September 1874)

Nonconformity, with its emphasis on educating through the Bible, the Chapel, and the Sunday School, helped to sustain people in their very rough, hard, and fraught daily life. There were fewer people in the St Beuno's area in the 1870s than in the 1990s, less movement, and villages were self-contained.

I have always looked on myself as half Welsh and so I warm to them.... I ought to say that the Welsh have the reputation also of being covetous and immoral: I add this to forestall your saying it, for, as I say, I warm to them – and in different degrees to all the Celts.
(Hopkins to his mother, 20 September 1874)

Because of the onerous farm-duties, sons seldom left home, often remaining unmarried, while there were also numerous daughters in the farmhouses whose housekeeping duties had kept them as spinsters. There was little extra money for wives. And so there was inbreeding, noticeable in faces and build, and even incest; intelligence suffered. In the big houses servants had little contact except with fellow-servants.

The Welsh round are very civil and respectful but do not much come to us and those who are converted are for the most part not very stanch. They are much swayed by ridicule. Wesleyanism is the popular religion. They are said to have a turn for religion, especially what excites outward fervour, and more refinement and pious feeling than the English peasantry but less steadfast-ness and sincerity.

(Hopkins to his mother, 20 September 1874)

The sparsity and generalised quality of Hopkins's comments on his Welsh neighbours show what little contact he had with any-one outside his own, essentially non-Welsh, community, and how – with very few exceptions – he could retain an idyllic picture of his surroundings during the whole of his three-year stay at St Beuno's.

I am trying a little Welsh. It is complicated but euphonious and regular. People think it has no vowels but just the contrary is true: it is almost all vowels and they run off the tongue like oil by diphthongs and by triphthongs – there are 20 of the latter and nearly 30 of the former.

(Hopkins to his mother, 20 September 1874)

There were two local social levels: the indigenous Welsh and the landed families. Both would speak Welsh, but the language was already dying out among the landed classes, with their circles of friends, the new North Wales coastal resorts populated largely by Lancashire immigrants, and railway travel now available to London. But Welsh was going strong in chapels, Sunday schools, and the weekly *seiat*, the fellowship meeting on Wednesday evenings, in the schoolroom attached to the chapel, where the group would discuss in Welsh, to a quite high intellectual standard, the previous Sunday's religious lessons. There were also numerous *eisteddfodau*.

Very bright and clear. I was with Mr. Rickaby on the hill above the house. All the landscape had a beautiful liquid cast of blue. Many-coloured smokes in the valley, grey from the Denbigh lime-kiln, yellow and lurid from two kilns perhaps on the shoul-ders of a hill, blue from a bonfire, and so on.

(Hopkins's journal, 24 September 1874)

The Roman Catholics of the district all went to St Beuno's chapel, which would be open every day for confessions and prayer. The next Roman Catholic churches were some distance away – Pantasaph and Holywell. Holywell was a very big Roman Catholic centre; from the famine years of the 1840s onwards there were many Irish Catholics, and the Irish element was very strong in Holywell. Many of these would be employed in the coal and lead mines. Some would settle in the area hoping for an opportunity to go off to North America: from the nearby docks at Mostyn ships went to Canadian ports such as Toronto and Montreal, and often the Irish would work their way across.

> Afterwards a lovely sunset of rosy juices and creams and combs; the combs I mean scattered floating bats or rafts or racks above, the creams / the strew and bed of the sunset, passing north and south or rather north only into grey marestail and brush along the horizon to the hills. Afterwards the rosy field of the sundown turned gold and the slips and creamings in it stood out like brands, with jots of purple. A sodden twilight over the valley and foreground all below, holding the corner-hung maroon-grey diamonds of ploughfields to one keeping but allowing a certain glare in the green of the near tufts of grass.
> (Hopkins's journal, 24 September 1874)

The district was notable for its profusion of crab-apples. There was no need to plant them in gardens, as they were in many hedges, coloured from deep red to butter-yellow. But the farmers did not use the hedge-fruits as they were costly in sugar, which – particularly if it was refined – at that time would be comparatively expensive.

> At rising I saw a long slender straight river of dull white cloud rolling down all the bed of the Clwyd from as far as I could look up the valley to the sea, in height perhaps twice as high as the Cathedral tower. Its outline rose and fell regularly in low or shallow waves or swellings like smooth knots in a bamboo and these swellings seemed not to be upwards only but also to bulge every way, encroaching on the fields as well. I could also see that it had a flaky or vertebrated make, the flakes leaning forward and curling and falling over a little. St. Asaph with the tower and trees and other spots appeared in grey washes at thinnings or openings of the mist. – At that time it was dull but cleared to a lovely

day – we have been having indeed a second summer –, but in the evening a fog came suddenly on and then cleared again.
(Hopkins's journal, 27 September 1874)

There were many squirrels, not (as now) grey, but all red. They would not last long: the grey squirrels came in about fifty years ago and killed off the red by stealing their food.

With Bodoano to Caerwys wood, a beautiful place. The day being then dark and threatening we walked some time under a grey light more charming than sunshine falling through boughs and leaves.
(Hopkins's journal, 28 September 1874)

Colours in nature were more widespread and intense in the 1870s. Hedges had some evergreen, especially holly and beech, so that even in winter there were several contrasting colours, particularly when set against the grey, lichen-studded dry walls.

Fresh firecoal chestnut-falls.
('Pied Beauty')

Bright and beautiful day. Crests of snow could be seen on the mountains. Barraud and I walked over to Holywell and bathed at the well and returned very joyously.
(Hopkins's journal, 8 October 1874)

The district was noted for its large number of bright orange foxes. Rabbits were far more numerous than nowadays, and people relied on them for meat.

The b[isho]p came, so we got a half holiday and I went with Rickaby to Cwm. We came back by the woods on the Rhuallt [hill] and the view was so like Ribblesdale from the fells that you might have thought you were there. The sky was iron grey and the valley, full of Welsh charm and graceful sadness, all in grave colours lay like a painted napkin.
(Hopkins's journal, 12 October 1874)

There were many bats in the district, nesting in roof-spaces and caves. At dusk you could hear their squeaking. At that period they were not protected, as now, but considered a nuisance, with their droppings and carrying germs. There was a lot of folklore and superstition about bats in the district.

> I was there [on the Rhuallt] again with Purbrick, at the scaffolding which is left as a mark of the survey at the highest point. We climbed on this and looked round: it was a fresh and delightful sight. The day was rainy and a rolling wind; parts of the landscape, as the Orms' Heads, were blotted out by rain.
> (Hopkins's journal, 19 October 1874)

> As when here a sheet of white rain coming from the sea blots out first the Orms' Heads on Moel Hiraddug, then spreads mile after mile, from hill to hill, from square to square of the fields, along the Vale of Clwyd, so the refreshment of the barley bread was spreading through that multitude.
> (from the undelivered part of Hopkins's Dominical sermon, on the miracle of the loaves and fishes)

> The clouds westwards were a pied piece – sail-coloured brown and milky blue; a dun yellow tent of rays opened upon the skyline far off.
> (Hopkins's journal, 19 October 1874)

> Glory be to God for dappled things –
> For skies of couple-colour as a brinded cow.
> ('Pied Beauty')

> Cobalt blue was poured on the hills bounding the valley of the Clwyd and far in the south spread a bluish damp, but all the nearer valley was showered with tapered diamond flakes of fields in purple and brown and green.
> (Hopkins's journal, 19 October 1874)

With so much more wild fruit and nuts to sustain it, bird-life in Hopkins's time would be much richer than now.

> As kingfishers catch fire, dragonflies draw flame.
> ('As kingfishers catch fire')

> ....I hear the lark ascend,
>   His rash-fresh re-winded new-skeined score
>   In crisps of curl off wild winch whirl, and pour

And pelt music, till none's to spill nor spend.
   ('The Sea and the Skylark')

The lark's song, which from his height gives the impression ... of
something falling to the earth and not vertically quite but trick-
lingly or wavingly, something as a skein of silk ribbed by having
been tightly wound on a narrow card or a notched holder ... the
laps or folds are the notes or short measures and bars of them.
The same is called a score in the musical sense of score and this
score is 'writ upon a liquid sky trembling to welcome it', only
not horizontally. The lark in wild glee races the reel round, pay-
ing or dealing out and down the turns of the skein ... right to the
... ground, where it lies in a heap, ... or rather is all wound off on
to another winch ... in Fancy's eye by the moment the bird
touches earth and so is ready for a fresh unwinding at the next
flight.
   (explanation of 'The Sea and the Skylark', letter to Bridges,
   November 1882)

Looking up along a white churchtower I caught a lovely sight –
a flock of seagulls wheeling and sailing high up in the air,
sparkles of white as bright as snowballs in the vivid blue.
   (letter to his mother, 2 March 1876)

      ... dapple-dawn-drawn Falcon, in his riding
   Of the rolling level underneath him steady air, and striding
High there, how he rung upon the rein of a wimpling wing
In his ecstacy!
   ('The Windhover')

Teevo cheevo cheevio chee:
O where, what can that be?
Weedio – weedio: there again!
So tiny a trickle of song-strain.
   ('The Woodlark')

      I whirled out wings that spell
And fled with a fling of the heart to the heart of the Host.
My heart, but you were dovewinged, I can tell,
      Carrier-witted.
   ('The Wreck of the Deutschland', st. 3)

Not that the sweet-fowl, song-fowl, needs no rest –

Why, hear him, hear him babble and drop down to his nest.
  ('The Caged Skylark')

Through the velvety wind V-winged
To the nest's nook I balance and buoy
With a sweet joy of a sweet joy,
Sweet, of a sweet, of a sweet joy
Of a sweet – a sweet – sweet – joy.
  ('The Woodlark')

                    ... My heart in hiding
Stirred for a bird, – the achieve of, the mastery of the thing!
Brute beauty and valour and act, oh, air, pride, plume....
  ('The Windhover')

                    .... thrush
Through the echoing timber does so rinse and wring
The ear, it strikes like lightnings to hear him sing.
  ('Spring')

                    ... the Holy Ghost over the bent
World broods with warm breast and with ah! bright wings.
  ('God's Grandeur')

There were many handsome buzzards, with huge wing-spans. In autumn the second clutch of pheasants would be dashing all over the roads, not knowing what to do with each other, with male pheasants striding around officiously, and the females anxiously trying to control their broods. The fields around Cefn would be full of pheasant chicks – in some there might be forty or fifty. Occasionally the dull refectory menu would include partridge, shot by the bailiff of Ty-Mawr.

> Walking with Wm. Splaine we saw a vast multitude of starlings making an unspeakable jangle. They would settle in a row of trees; then, one tree after another, rising at a signal they looked like a cloud of specks of black snuff or powder struck up from a brush or broom or shaken from a wig; then they would sweep round in whirlwinds – you could see the nearer and farther bow of the rings by the size and blackness; many would be in one phase at once, all narrow black flakes hurling round, then in another; then they would fall upon a field and so on. Splaine

wanted a gun: then 'there it would rain meat' he said. I thought they must be full of enthusiasm and delight hearing their cries and stirring and cheering one another.
(Hopkins's journal, 8 November 1874)

There was a dovecote in the St Beuno's grounds, where there were fan-tails, a pair of which, during Hopkins's stay there, were given as a present to a convent in York.

Flake-doves sent floating forth at a farmyard scare.
('The Starlight Night')

Late autumn was the time for slaughtering pigs, with professional pig-killers going around the district, their route signalled by ghastly squealings. Every part of the pig was used – for sausages, chitterlings, brawn, Bath chaps, and black puddings; all these many foods had to be consumed immediately. The only part of the pig not to be consumed straightaway but to be stored was the ham, which was salted in a big bath and then hung up to dry in the kitchen on hooks suspended from the rafters. There were feasts when local pigs were killed. Strict nonconformist tradition, or the presence of a strange black-coated foreign-looking Jesuit, might have put a damper on festivities, but there were local fairs as well. In late autumn also there were smells of burning leaves everywhere, all over the St Beuno's grounds and in the farms roundabout.

Bitter north wind, hail and sleet. On the hills snow lying and the mountains covered from head to foot. But they could scarcely be seen till next day ... which was fine and clear. I went with Mr. Hughes up Moel y Parch, from the top of which we had a noble view, but the wind was very sharp. Snowdon and all the range reminded me of the Alps: they looked like a stack of rugged white flint, specked and streaked with black, in many places chiselled and channelled. Home by Caerwys wood, where we saw two beautiful swans, as white as they should be, restlessly steering and 'canting' in the water and following us along the shore: one of them several times, as if for vexation, caught and gnawed at the stone quay of the sluice close under me.
(Hopkins's journal, 11 November 1874)

A sombre and poignant event was All Souls' Day – a gloomy

feast to take you into the darkness of winter; the onset of a long, dark time for the district, with very little light, only candlelight. The gloom would be likely to be heightened in an institution, with the studied formality of its meals, and where one gloomy person could affect the rest. Everywhere in the Vale of Clwyd would seem shut down for the long winter, with Masses and ceremonies for relief. But there were magnificent large fires, with wonderfully-smelling pine – unless your room was unfortunate enough to have lukewarm central heating.

> Away in the loveable west,
> On a pastoral forehead of Wales,
> I was under a roof here, I was at rest.
> ('The Wreck of the Deutschland', st. 24)

St Beuno's is perfectly placed for wonderful winter views over the Snowdonian range, particularly when the sun is sparkling. You could always tell if it had snowed in the night because of the reflected light and the snow-stillness. There was snow for almost the whole of winter, but it was most beautiful when there was ice on top of the snow: then it would be crisp and unearthly. The Vale of Clwyd can look very lush, even in winter. St Beuno's is just below the snow-line, so that during the winter snows the college grounds may sometimes have stayed green, and the residents could have looked behind them at the snow higher up on Maenefa, and ahead at the Snowdon range across the vale. To the right of this range shimmering blue snow and ice-caps would last the winter, while immediately in front would be the placid landscape of the vale, with the sea in all its moods away to the right. At this time of year skating was one of the few opportunities for them to let their hair down.

> All the valley is under snow. It freezes and there has been skating today – tempered by catastrophes and wettings to the middle – on a lake called Llyn Helyg. Hitherto we had floods of rain.
> (Hopkins to his mother, 18 December 1874)

> Then off, off forth on swing,
> As a skate's heel sweeps smooth on a bow-bend.
> ('The Windhover')

It would be quite a hard life in winter, dark or grey, and not easy to get out of the college. When walks were possible, they would not meet many people. It is likely that any sense of oppression would be increased in winter, though there would be lovely storm-clouds over Snowdonia, and what has been described as '*Götterdämmerung* weather'. Hopkins stayed at St Beuno's for the Christmas of his first year in Wales. Normally a family celebration, it became a sad occasion if you were not going away: reassurance was needed, and there was no way of getting it. A second glass of wine on the feast-days was extraordinary enough to be commented on in the house journal; once there was even champagne. Occasionally another Jesuit house might send gifts of turkey, hare, pheasant or venison. Once there were grapes. During Christmas vacations there were spelling-bees, a recently-introduced American parlour-game at which Hopkins excelled, and he described a holiday entertainment in which 'glees and songs are very nicely sung, pieces are read from Dickens, George Eliot etc, scenes from Shakespeare, speeches, poems and so on'.

> The Vale has been looking very beautiful. A neighbouring lake or llyn has been a sheet of very glassy ice and given very good skating, but I have let the opportunity slip. Now a thaw has set in. Yesterday I bathed in St. Winefred's Well, which, as it is always at the same temperature, was lukewarm and smoked in the frosty air.
> (Hopkins to his mother, 27 December 1879)

There would be a lack of familial warmth and intimacy in the St Beuno's community. People have a need for intimacy, and male religious orders had a superstitious fear of women and of intimacy with women; cats would provide a useful way of displaying affection for a group of men with nobody but each other, and there was Vesta, a watch-dog mastiff, who had sometimes won prizes at the Rhyl Show. Within the college community there would be an amount of gossip, sometimes malicious, and Chinese whispers. On a daily basis there would probably be fighting over who got *The Times*, and constant searching of the Births, Marriages, and Deaths columns (many Jesuits had been born into the higher ranks of society).

Heavy fall of snow. Hitherto much rain, with floods in the valley.

After this snow and frost till the 2nd of January, I think, after
which it was mild and towards the end of that month the birds
were singing.
(Hopkins's journal, December 1874-January 1875)

The pace of life in the countryside around St Beuno's would be
erratic, and depend on the time of year. In the winter there would be
long periods when the snow or frost meant that no work could be
done, and the water supply could be interrupted.

> ... a water in a well, to a poise, to a pane,
> But roped with, always, all the way down from the tall
>   Fells or flanks of the voel, a vein.
>   ('The Wreck of the Deutschland', st. 4)

The farmhouses would have the family at one end and the cattle
at the other, with the dividing wall conducting the animal heat. The
smells from these long-houses were very strong in winter, until the
animals were let out. The cows would cavort like lunatics when first
let loose – there was fear lest they break their necks.

> I admire thee, master of the tides,
>   Of the Yore-flood, of the year's fall;
> The recurb and the recovery of the gulf's sides,
>   The girth of it and the wharf of it and the wall;
> Stanching, quenching ocean of a motionable mind.
>   ('The Wreck of the Deutschland', st. 32)

Nowadays you can fill the house with supermarket flowers, but
there was nothing in the 1870s to lighten up the house in winter,
except for gloomy Victorian house plants, such as aspidistras and
poinsettias. In Hopkins's day much was made of holly and mistle-
toe, both plentiful in the district.

> I wonder at Orion rising through the clear night, even though
> the bright moon is close at hand and presses more heavily on the
> small stars nor allows them to shine with her. Yet I marvel how
> this Orion grows up the sky and how it gleams with its own fire,
> which a force that is not its own makes bright in the heavens,
> while its soft lustre comes and goes: why, you would think that
> some winds had the power to whirl its seven star-points round
> and round. I marvel too that the breezes and the tepid South

wind are wafted so pleasantly, and that winter and the first
Kalends which the new year keeps are so warm, for from that
day which has just set, the fairest in the year, we say the days (of
the year) take their start.

(translation of the opening of '*Miror surgentem*', a Latin poem
composed by Hopkins one New Year's day, probably 1874)

Food would be severely limited in variety over winter – a few
apples and pears out of the store as an occasional treat. Even butter
and milk would be in short supply over the winter, the calving in
early spring preventing much milk.

> .... even in weariest wintry hour
> Of New Year's month or surly Yule
> Furred snows, charged tuft above tuft, tower.
> ('Penmaen Pool')

> A released shower, let flash to the shire, not a lightning of fire hard-
> hurled.
> ('The Wreck of the Deutschland', st. 34)

The hens tended to give up laying eggs over winter, going into a
moult; hens need light. Epiphany was an exciting start to the year,
when things started happening – such as the first snowdrops.

> I kiss my hand
> To the stars, lovely-asunder
> Starlight, wafting him out of it; and
> Glow, glory in thunder;
> Kiss my hand to the dappled-with-damson west.
> ('The Wreck of the Deutschland', st. 5)

The first signs of spring would come very early – at the end of
January. St Beuno's is sheltered by the steep hillside at its back, and
there would be a succession of spring bulbs, one variety after
another. And the trees would be changing from their winter skeleton to the first yellow-green. After the snowdrops came early members of the buttercup family.

> ... nature is never spent;
> There lives the dearest freshness deep down things;

And though the last lights from the black West went,
O morning, on the brown brink eastwards, springs.
(early version of 'God's Grandeur')

Sheep which had been out in the fields over winter would be brought into folds for lambing. By the beginning of February the winter stillness would have been replaced by lambing sounds: the bleating of new-born lambs, and the baaing of their mothers. The lambs would all come early in the year, and not spread out, as they are now.

> The day was bright, the sun sparkling through a frostfog which made the distance dim and the stack of Denbigh hill, as we came near, dead mealy grey against the light: the castle ruins, which crown the hill, were punched out in arches and half arches by bright breaks and eyelets of daylight.
> (Hopkins's journal, 4 February 1875)

In February were heard the noises of rooks, crows, and ravens (many more then than now). The barn- and tawny-owl cries changed from their eerie winter chorus, apparently commenting on disaster, to individual, very different, mating calls, from single trees.

> A party of us set out for Moel Fammau, the highest of the hills bounding the valley and distant as the crow flies about nine miles. There stands on it what remains of the Jubilee Tower erected in honour of George III's 50th year of royalty, an ugly and trumpery construction, makebelieve-massive but so frail that it was blown over by the gale that wrecked the Royal Charter, and it cumbers the hilltop and interrupts the view. As we walked along the hills towards it the valley looked more charming and touching than ever: in its way there can hardly be in the world anything to beat the Vale of Clwyd. The day was then threatening and clouded, the sea and distant hills brimmed with purple, clouds trailing low, the landscape clear but sober, the valley though so verdant appeared of a pale blush-colour from the many red sandstone fresh-ploughed fields. Clarke and I made one of the only two couples that reached Moel Fammau. When we had come down into the valley the day became very beautiful.
> (Hopkins to his mother, describing Shrove Tuesday 1876)

We live on a hillside of the beautiful valley of the Clwyd, but

now the other side of the valley vanishes in mist and the ground
is deep in snow.... It was yesterday waistdeep in the drifts.
(Hopkins to Robert Bridges, 20-22 February 1875)

Now many more sounds, such as that of foxes barking like dogs.
In the last days of February there would be the mating cries of many
birds.

> Thrush's eggs look little low heavens.
> ('Spring')

> That cordial air made those kind people a hood
>   All over, as a bevy of eggs the mothering wing
>   Will, or mild nights the new morsels of Spring.
> ('In the Valley of the Elwy')

> We have had very sharp frost with bitter north winds, but today
> the wind is changed. I am much annoyed not to have seen the
> total eclipse of the moon last night. I saw it only when it was
> three parts over, the moon being dazzling bright and the shadow
> brown. Someone on the spot excused himself for not letting us
> know sooner by saying it was in all the almanacks. People who
> one wd. have thought were better informed were letting off wild
> remarks about disks and heavenly bodies and what not.
> (Hopkins to his mother, 1 March 1877)

There would be the excitement of ploughing and sowing.
Throughout the year the fields would be a patchwork: ploughed
fields, hay, cereals, and the staple root-crops (now gone) of man-
golds, turnips, swedes, and of course potatoes. No modern maize,
rape, or mustard.

> Sheer plod makes plough down sillion/ Shine.
> ('The Windhover')

> Look, the elf-rings! look at the out-round earnest eyes!
> The grey lawns cold where quaking gold-dew lies!
> (early version of 'The Starlight Night', sent by Hopkins to his
> mother for her fifty-sixth birthday, 3 March 1877)

When they went a walk they could find a sheltered nook where,
on pushing the foliage away, they would see the first primroses, as

Hopkins did at the end of February 1877.

> March-bloom, like on mealed-with-yellow sallows!
>   ('The Starlight Night')

> Let him easter in us, be a dayspring to the dimness of us, be a crim-
> son-cresseted east.
>   ('The Wreck of the Deutschland', st. 35)

About the middle of April the lay brother in charge of brewing beer changed his role, as it was assumed that there was enough beer to last until October, in order to concentrate on spring-cleaning, which also involved a large amount of white- and colour-washing. From February onwards there were good hauls of fish, particularly of trout in the Elwy, caught by Theologian anglers, known as the 'Dufferhood', who would sometimes be away from the college by half-past six in the morning for a day's fishing. The biggest fish caught while Hopkins was at St Beuno's was one of four-and-a-quarter pounds.

> Rose-moles all in stipple upon trout that swim.
>   ('Pied Beauty')

> Such a backward spring I cannot remember. Now things begin
> to look greener and the cuckoo may be heard but our climate on
> the hillside is a touch Arctic. I have recovered from a cold I
> caught lately and am well but for daily indigestion, which
> makes study much harder and our shadowless glaring walks to
> my eyes very painful.
>   (Hopkins to his mother, 24 April 1874)

> Look, look: a May-mess, like on orchard boughs!
>   ('The Starlight Night')

> For how to the heart's cheering
>   The down-dugged ground-hugged grey
> Hovers off, the jay-blue heavens appearing
>   Of pied and peeled May!
>   ('The Wreck of the Deutschland', st. 26)

> Lovely the woods, waters, meadows, combes, vales,
> All the air things wear that build this world of Wales.
>   ('In the Valley of the Elwy', 23 May 1877)

GERARD MANLEY HOPKINS IN WALES

We killed a great big snake in a cornfield but it was not an adder
and we might have spared it if we had had time to think.
(Hopkins to his mother, 10 June 1875)

A contemporary of Hopkins's at St Beuno's estimated that out of
the 1,800 flowering plants in Great Britain, 'probably a diligent col-
lector would be able to show 1,200 gathered within the bounds of
our district'. On one June walk of an hour along lanes within two
miles of St Beuno's I myself passed these on the roadside: bluebells
varying in colour from deep purple to white, with several intermediate shades of sky-blue and grey-blue – whole woods could be seen
which could be called 'bluebell woods'; buttercups, daisies, dande-
lions, the slender yellow horseshoe vetch and several other vetches,
including the bush vetch, red and white and zigzag clovers, greater
stitchwort, common and dog violets, germander speedwell, lesser
bindweed, druce, several shades of cornflower, the delicately blue
scabious, wild irises, the slender tormentil, creeping cinquefoil,
common agrimony, wood garlic, early purple orchids, the beautiful
blue-purple flower of the ground ivy, many kinds of veronica, wood
and common forget-me-nots, pinks, the lesser periwinkle, the hairy-
stemmed blue bugle (these last two Tennyson liked and wrote
about), primroses, cowslips, knapweeds, different kinds of willow
herb, sorrel, sweet briars and dog-roses, woundworts, wild sage and
thyme, and vast amounts of common cow parsley, *anthriscus
sylvestris*, which Hopkins called 'fretty chervil'. There are also much
rarer plants in the district: *Flora Britannica* (1996) reports that a five-
leaved herb-paris still grows in the same wood near Caerwys, Coed
Maesmyan, where it had been noted in the seventeenth century by
Sir John Salusbury.

In my Welsh days, in my salad days.
(Hopkins to Bridges, from Stonyhurst, Lancashire, November
1882)

Wild Wales breathes poetry.
(Hopkins to Canon Dixon, from Tremadoc, September 1886)

Wales, always to me a mother of Muses.
(Hopkins to Bridges, from Tremadoc, October 1886)

72

I have just returned from a very reviving fortnight or so in North Wales, the true Arcadia of wild beauty.
(Hopkins to Coventry Patmore, from Dublin, October 1886)

So that in this valley, St. Asaph would be where the Jordan enters the valley; Bethsaida Julias would be Rhuddlan; Capharnaum would be near Llannefydd standing high; but Bethsaida near Henllan; Tiberias would be Denbigh; Chorozain might be Bodfari; and the place of the miracle seems to have been at the north end of the lake, on the east side of the Jordan, as it might be at this very spot where we are now upon the slope of Maenefa.
(Dominical sermon given by Hopkins in March 1877, in the refectory of St Beuno's)

I awoke in the midsummer not-to-call night,   in the white and
    the walk of the morning:
The moon, dwindled and thinned to the fringe   of a fingernail held
    to the candle,
Or paring of paradisaical fruit,   lovely in waning but lustreless,
Stepped from the stool, drew back from the barrow,   of dark Maenefa
    the mountain.
('Moonrise June 19 1876')

Flesh falls within sight of us, we, though our flower the same,
        Wave with the meadow, forget that there must
The sour scythe cringe, and the blear share come.
('The Wreck of the Deutschland', st. 11)

In Hopkins's day, corn was not cut, as it is now, when it was just ripe, but was allowed to go through several stages of deepening colour. In the 1870s corn was also softer, unlike the modern varieties with their purposely stiff stalks. Softer corn meant that the growing crop would sway more, and be more likely to be blown down or sideways in strong winds.

The blue wheat-acre is underneath
And the corn is corded and shoulders its sheaf,
The ear in milk, lush the sash,
And crush-silk poppies aflash.
('The Woodlark', 5 July 1876)

Haymaking, closely followed by the harvest, was a communal occasion, when all would help each other against their great enemy, the weather. Young women and children (it was quite usual for them to be given time off school) would help the men, who were armed with lethal pitchforks and long, wide, wooden rakes.

> And down ... the furrow dry
> Sunspurge and oxeye
> And lace-leaved lovely
> Foam-tuft fumitory.
>   ('The Woodlark', 5 July 1876)

The older women, picturesque in long dresses and wearing aprons, possibly shawls, and the mandatory bonnets for protection against the sun, would sustain the labour-force in the cornfields with huge baskets covered in white cloths and containing doorstep sandwiches of home-made bread, cheese, and pickles, bara brith, wedges of fruit-cake and Welsh cakes, all washed down with gallons of sweet tea or buttermilk. (On some farms there would be cider, but nonconformism was strong enough in these parts to prevent much 'drinking'.) When cutting corn, there would be the promise of rabbit pie, the machines going round in decreasing circles, while men with shotguns waited for the creatures who were all chased into the middle of the field. After cutting, the corn was stooked in sheaves, bound with straw, and left to dry, and to the reapers and gleaners. Children of the 1870s must have had as much fun as later generations in the straw or hay, or playing 'house' among the stooks, and vying for the honour of helping on top of the hay- or corn-stack, to get it into a weatherproof state.

> Summer ends now; now, barbarous in beauty, the stooks rise
> Around; up above, what wind-walks! what lovely behaviour
> Of silk-sack clouds! has wilder, wilful-wavier
> Meal-drift moulded ever and melted across skies?
>   ('Hurrahing in Harvest', Vale of Clwyd, 1 September 1877)

Harvest Thanksgiving services would have been just that – the countryside was by and large self-sufficient in food, and it mattered a very great deal how good the harvests were.

THE YEAR AT ST BEUNO'S

Men go by me, whom either beauty bright
   In mould or mind or what not else makes rare:
   They rain against our much-thick and marsh air
Rich beams, till death or distance buys them quite.
   ('The Lantern out of Doors', St Beuno's, 1877)

No sooner were we among the Welsh hills than I saw the hawks flying and other pleasant sights soon to be seen no more.
   (Hopkins to his father, 15 August 1877, two months before he took his last look at St Beuno's, and set out for Mount St Mary's College, near Sheffield, from where he wrote:

The air is never once clear in this country, not to see distances as in Wales.)

Five
'The most wearisome work':
Brother Hopkins, Theology Student

When he started on his theology studies at St Beuno's Hopkins had already spent six years in the Society of Jesus. For two years from September 1868 he had been a novice at Roehampton, near London; then for the next three years he had studied philosophy at St Mary's Hall, Stonyhurst, in Lancashire; and for the academic year 1873-4 he had taught Jesuit 'Junior' students at Roehampton again.

The main purpose of the noviceship was to train the young Jesuit in humility and 'that spirit of implicit and unquestioning obedience which is the aim of the Society of Jesus to cultivate more than any other virtue in her sons' (*Clarke*, 219). A contemporary of Hopkins's wrote that

> The routine of monotonous and often apparently useless employments has for its object to foster the habit of what is rightly called blind obedience. The novice is taught to obey his superior without ever questioning the wisdom of the order given; the perfection of Jesuit obedience includes not only the obedience of the will, so that he does what is commanded promptly, bravely, and thoroughly, but also an obedience of the judgment, so that he regards what is commanded as the best thing possible for him.... It is the habit, the difficult habit of abstaining from any mental criticism of the order given that is the distinctive feature of the obedience of the Society of Jesus.
> (*Clarke*, ibid.)

It is easy to see how this rigorous denial of merit to original and impulsive thought and feeling fitted in with Hopkins's undergraduate indulgence in self-mortification and religious scrupulousness, but hard to envisage how his various submerged creative impulses would be able to find fertile ground in which to grow and blossom. Being governed by such aims, and by a very closely packed daily timetable, enabled the institution to flourish at the expense of the individual.

One example of how the constant scrutiny of motives encouraged by his training had directly hindered creative opportunity is the six-months' custody-of-the-eyes penance undergone by Hopkins in the novitiate from January to July 1869. For a poet who used his eyes to such remarkable effect such punitive puritanism could only be anathema, whatever rationale sanctioned it. His personal writing also suffered greatly. On his first Long Retreat, in mid-September 1868, he had vowed: 'Henceforth I keep no regular weather-journal but only notes' (J, 189), and his journal, which at Oxford he had used to record his everyday thoughts on a wide variety of subjects, he now limited severely, writing in it only occasionally, and restricting its subject-matter. His journal during the two years of his noviceship covers only twelve printed pages (J, 189-200), while during his Swiss holiday, which had lasted less than a month immediately before he joined the Jesuits, he had filled sixteen (J, 168-184). And, as far as we know, Hopkins did not write any poetry during his two years in the novitiate. In order to fit in with the severe restrictions of his training, he was purposely suppressing his natural compulsion to write.

Even the official 'recreation' period each day was over-solemn and carefully controlled to a chilling degree:

> Towards the end of the recreation the porter looked at his watch, clapped his hands for silence, and then announced, 'Brother So-and-So will give us a *pia fabula*.' Someone had been deputed to prepare a short, edifying story, an incident in the life of a saint or something similar, to deliver to the assembled novices before we went down to the chapel for Litanies or a benediction service. Most of these pious anecdotes were rather emotional, often incredible, but not consciously humorous or witty. Satire was frowned on in the noviceship.
> (OM, 55-6)

The only regular breaks in the monotony of the novice's week were teaching catechism classes in local churches and taking part in dirges.

From the noviceship Hopkins had gone into the first year of the 'Philosophy' course at St Mary's Hall, Stonyhurst, which consisted largely of mathematics, and pure and applied logic, while in his second and third years he was taught 'psychology, ethics, metaphysics, general and special, cosmology and natural theology' (*Clarke*, 221). The English Province of the Society of Jesus had no competent teachers of 'Philosophy' from its own ranks, and so Hopkins's teachers were undistinguished professors from Germany or Italy who had not published anything. All Hopkins's recorded comments on the course were negative. In his first year he told his friend Baillie that he was 'going through a hard course of scholastic logic ... which takes all the fair part of the day and leaves one fagged at the end for what remains. This makes the life painful to nature' (*L3*, 234). In his third year he wrote: 'I am here for another year and now they are having at me with ethics and mechanics. Today is a whole holiday: I spent a miserable morning over formulas for the lever' (*L3*, 234).

The one bright aspect of his three years in the Philosophate was Hopkins's joyful recording of his relationships with flora, fauna, and the general scenery of the Lancashire countryside. In spite of his vow to curtail the importance of journal-writing in his Jesuit life, Hopkins's compulsion to express himself poetically and analytically surfaced during his time at Stonyhurst. While his few attempts at writing verse are restrained and forgettable pieces written for special religious occasions, his prose descriptions show his poetic facility for endless metaphorical expansion from the simplest basic images. On 21 April 1871 he recorded:

> the sky a beautiful grained blue, silky lingering clouds in flat-bottomed loaves, others a little browner in ropes or in burly-shouldered ridges swanny and lustrous, more in the Zenith stray packs of a sort of violet paleness. White-rose cloud formed fast, not in the same density – some caked and swimming in a wan whiteness, the rest soaked with the blue and like the leaf of a flower held against the light and diapered out by the worm or veining of deeper blue between rosette and rosette. Later/ moulding, which brought rain: in perspective it was vaulted in

very regular ribs with fretting between: but these are not ribs; they are a 'wracking' install made of these two realities – the frets which are scarves of rotten cloud bellying upwards and drooping at their ends and shaded darkest at the brow or tropic where they double to the eye, and the whiter field of sky shewing between: the illusion looking down the 'wagon' is complete. These swaths of fretted cloud move in rank, not in file.

(J, 207)

Several difficult characteristics of his later poems are apparent here, such as specialist vocabulary (the architectural: *diapered, moulding, vaulted, ribs, fretting*) or highly subjective imagery, long sentences, and syntax which proceeds by inspiration rather than planned logic.

There is a fine but difficult passage which must be the longest – and certainly the most extraordinary combination of subjective yet disciplined description – ever written about what human eyes can see when looking at a bunch of bluebells (J, 208-9); and he also gave a particularly remarkable account of a peacock with spread train:

It has a very regular warp, like a shell, in which the bird embays himself, the bulge being inwards below but the hollow inwards above, cooping him in and only opening towards the brim, where the feathers are beginning to rive apart. The eyes, which lie alternately when the train is shut, like scales or gadroons, fall into irregular rows when it is opened, and then it thins and darkens against the light, it loses the moistness and satin it has when in the pack but takes another/ grave and excessive splendour, and the outermost eyes, detached and singled, give with their corner fringes the suggestion of that inscape of the flowing cusped trefoil which is often effective in art.

At this point the description becomes both more joyful and more removed from the starting-object:

He shivers it when he first rears it and then again at intervals and when this happens the rest blurs and the eyes start forward – I have thought it looks like a tray or green basket or fresh-cut willow hurdle set all over with Paradise fruits cut through – first through a beard of golden fibre and then through wet flesh greener than greengages or purpler than grapes – or say that the knife had caught a tatter or flag of the skin and laid it flat across the flesh – and then within all a sluggish corner drop of black or purple oil.

(J, 209-10)

Quite apart from analyses of traditional pastoral subjects, such as flowers, trees, clouds, and weather effects, there are other passages which show that – in spite of puritanical promises and training – he had renewed his pre-Jesuit, purely secular, live interests in powerful vocabulary and dialect. There are accounts of everyday occurrences and domestic imagery, such as a lengthy description of the surface of a cup of evening cocoa, that recall his wonderful Swiss journal, and show that he was practising many kinds of aesthetic exercise which had nothing to do with his profession. The oft-quoted comment of Hopkins's when looking at a bluebell, 'I know the beauty of our Lord by it' (J, 199), is not only atypical of his journal but unique: on the evidence of his journal-writing he does *not* see God in Nature, which retains its own nature for him.

At St Beuno's the theologate curriculum was also anything but poetic:

Here the work is certainly hard, especially during the first two years. On three days in the week, the student who has passed successfully through his philosophical course has to attend two lectures in the morning and three in the afternoon. The morning lectures are on moral and dogmatic theology; and those in the afternoon on canon law or history, dogmatic theology, and Hebrew, the last for half an hour only. Besides this, on each of these afternoons there is held a circle or disputation.... In theology these disputations are as a rule fiercer and more searching than in the philosophical course.... In addition to these constant disputations there is held every three months a more solemn assembly of the same kind, at which the whole house is present and the rector presides, in which two of the students are chosen to defend for an hour continuously a number of theses against the attacks of all comers, the professors themselves included.

During the third and fourth years of the course of theology, lectures in Scripture are substituted for those on moral theology and Hebrew. At the end of the third year the young Jesuit (if a man of thirty-four or thirty-five can be accounted young) is

ordained priest, and during his last year his lectures are fewer, and he has privately to prepare himself for a general examination in theology, on which depends in great measure whether he has the grade of a professed father in the Society or the lower degree of what is called a 'spiritual coadjutor'.
(*Clarke*, 223-4)

Every Tuesday evening there was held in addition the 'case of conscience', in which two Theologians gave prepared solutions to imaginary problems, while all the students were expected to contribute.

Hopkins's teachers were the Rector, Fr James Jones (an Irishman whom Hopkins already knew), Fr John Morris, an Englishman, a Venetian, Fr Emilio Perini, and a German, Fr Bernhard Tepe. The main theologian studied, to the exclusion of most others, was Suarez, about whom Hopkins was less than enthusiastic: 'He is a man of vast volume of mind, but without originality or brilliancy; he treats everything satisfactorily, but you never remember a phrase of his, the manner is nothing' (*L2*, 95). Twentieth-century commentators agree that 'the sacred science' of theology was both narrow and 'at a low ebb' among English Roman Catholics at this time. As with the previous 'Philosophy' course, Hopkins's comments show weariness and lack of enthusiasm for his studies: 'the close pressure of my theological studies leaves me time for hardly anything: the course is very hard, it must be said' (*L1*, 30-1). In June 1875, at the end of his first year of theology, he gave as excuse for not writing to his family 'the pressure of the approaching examination makes me unwilling to do more correspondence than necessary' (*L3*, 133-4). And in March 1877, he wrote to his mother: 'I am to be examined in moral theology to see whether I am fit to hear confessions. Going over moral theology over and over again and in a hurry is the most wearisome work and tonight at all events I am so tired I am good for nothing' (*L3*, 143). Only a month later he wrote: 'I am very very tired, yes "a thousand times and yet a thousand times" and "scarce can go or creep"' (*L1*, 33).

As some sort of relief from the wearisome and sadly unbalanced round of theology there were walks on Sunday and Tuesday afternoons. The students were not allowed to choose who were to be their companions, and so the walks were referred to as 'lotteries'. In addition every Thursday was a recreation day, when sandwiches were available but not money. On Sundays two sermons were preached, one, called the 'tone', in the refectory to the community while they were eating, and the other, the 'dominical', at evening Mass.

One of these dominicals, on mid-Lent Sunday 11 March 1877, was delivered by Hopkins, and the text still exists (*S*, 225-33). The Gospel for the day was from John 6, on the Feeding of the Five Thousand. Hopkins took just one sentence for his sermon, 'Then Jesus said: "Make the men sit down"'. He started by conjuring up a Composition of Place, as Ignatius had taught his followers to do: 'Let us do as we are accustomed – return to the story, turn it over and dwell on it, go in mind to that time and in spirit to that place'; and to illustrate the setting of the Sea of Galilee drew a detailed comparison with the Clwyd Valley, so that 'Capharnaum would be near Llannefydd standing high', Bethsaida would be near Henllan, 'Tiberias would be Denbigh', and 'Chorozain might be Bodfari'. St Asaph would be where the river Jordan entered the valley. There were many other precise equivalent places or geographical features, too many for an audience, even one with the community's local knowledge, to take in without a detailed diagram. Hopkins made matters worse by suggesting an alternative method of imagining the place of the miracle, by extended simile:

> The lake is shaped something like a bean or something like a man's left ear; the Jordan enters at the top of the upper rim, it runs out at the end of the lobe or drop of the ear. One Bethsaida – Bethsaida Julias – stands by the Jordan as it were above the ear in the hair.... Tiberias on the tongue of flesh that stands out from the cheek into the hollow of the ear.

Hopkins so often in his sermons (as in his college lectures) seems unable to be concise; he will naturally elaborate until the congregation must have lost the thread and direction. And in this sermon there are several digressions, such as this bit of pedantry on the name 'Philip':

> Here, brethren, remark a mystery. Philip is a Greek, not a Jewish, name; it has a noble air; it suits noblemen, like Guy or

Marmaduke or Perceval – with us. It means fond of horses, proud of his stud; not fond as a groom is of the horse he grooms or a ploughman or coachman of his team but as a wealthy man is of his stud, his show of cost and wealth and pride. The name then means one who has an eye to the pomp and beauty of this world.

A few minutes further on Hopkins gave another unfortunate ramification, this time dithering over numbers, a curious idiosyncracy which sometimes surfaces in other writings of his:

> *Two hundred pennyworth of bread is not enough even for each to get a little.* Of course a penny in the Scripture means much more than a penny – a shilling say or more than that: £10 worth, he says, would not make a good meal and £10 was more than they had got. This was all his contemplation came to: to say what was *not enough*. He made, I do suppose, a correct reckoning; two hundred pennyworth would *not* have done for the poorest meal and besides they had not the money. But, dear brethren, this answer is even laughable. For if a man is appealed to about the price of a house, a field, a feast or at a public supper, anything, he may answer: It will cost £1000, £100, £10 or 10s. and he may add: That will cover it but that is more than you can afford, but is it not a singular, an unhelpful, an oddly unpractical answer to say £1000 is *not* enough for the house even without the garden; £100 is *not* enough for the field even without the sheds and buildings; £10 is *not* enough for the supper even without the wine? Who wants that kind of answer?

The enlargement from the sparse basic text is much too finicky, and the sermon is a product of the study rather than for the pulpit. Although Hopkins mentions his audience several times, there is little sense of his imagining a dialogue with their minds. To make matters worse, he repeated the phrase 'Make the men sit down' numerous times, so that it sounds like a comic chorus, rather than thoughtful embroidery. At the end of Hopkins's manuscript he added poignantly: 'People laughed at it prodigiously, I saw some of them roll on their chairs with laughter. This made me lose the thread, so that I did not deliver the last two paragraphs right but mixed things up. The last paragraph, in which *Make the men sit down* is often repeated, far from having a good effect, made them roll more than ever.'

At least the sermon was delivered in English; it should be remembered that a large part of Hopkins's theology course was conducted in Latin, and students were encouraged to keep up that dead language, because in some parts of the ecclesiastical world it was still considered the international means of communication.

That anachronistic and penitential way of life at St Beuno's has recently been described by a Jesuit as one of 'sustained uneventfulness', with Hopkins delaying sending letters back to Hampstead because he had nothing to write about. This 'static quality of theologate life', said Fr Thomas, was reflected in the entries in the Beadle's journal for Advent 1874:

> Dec. 11 Friday. As usual. Penances: Expos & Ben [Exposition and Benediction]. Fast-day Dinner 12.
> 12 Saturday. Schools [i.e. Lectures]. Missioners off to work.
> 13 Sunday. As usual: tone: walk: Ben: Debate: Dominical.
> 14 Monday. As usual: penances: missioners returned.
> 15 Tuesday. As usual: case: Fr Minister goes into retreat.
> 16 Wednesday. As usual: fast-day, dinner 12.
> 17 Thursday. Weekly recreation. No companies, 1 because Minister in retreat, 2 because snow on the ground.
> 18 Friday. As usual: Penances: Exhort: Expos & Ben. Fast Day.
> (*HTJ*, 162-3)

The Beadle's journal for New Year's Eve a fortnight later suggests that that particular occasion was less happy than most secular people's:

> Ben and Te Deum 7.30. The Te Deum was a most lamentable performance showing neglect of preparation. After supper an attempt was made to exhibit the Magic Lantern in the recreation-room: – there was a deficiency of light.
> (*HTJ*, 163)

The contrast between the Beadle's journal and Hopkins's graphically conveys the vast difference between Hopkins's professional and private lives:

> [4 February 1875] Denbigh is a taking picturesque town. Seen from here ... it is always beautiful. The limekiln under a quarried cliff on this side of the town is always sending out a white smoke

and this, and the greyer smoke of Denbigh, creeping up on the hill, what with sun and wind give fairy effects which are always changing.

The day was bright, the sun sparkling through a frostfog which made the distance dim and the stack of Denbigh hill, as we came near, dead mealy grey against the light: the castle ruins, which crown the hill, were punched out in arches and half arches by bright breaks and eyelets of daylight. We went up to the castle but not in: standing before the gateway I had an instress which only the true old work gives from the strong and noble inscape of the pointed arch. We went to eat our lunch to a corner opening by a stone stile upon a wilderness by which you get down to the town, under the outer wall, overgrown with ivy, bramble, and some graceful herb with glossy lush green sprays, something like celery.

(J, 262-3)

(The 'corner opening by a stone stile upon a wilderness' is there today as Hopkins described it, though the gateway arch has lost much by both decay and restoration in the last hundred or so years, and is difficult to recognise from Hopkins's description.)

On most Sunday evenings a debate was held just before supper. The subjects were carefully chosen, most being concerned with the Society's or the Roman Catholic church's political or doctrinal or social policies. Subjects while Hopkins was at St Beuno's included 'That Catholics should support the movement for the disestablishment of the Church of England', 'That the parochial clergy should interest themselves in the establishment of clubs and club-houses for the use of the Catholic working classes', and 'Painting is a more powerful aid to religion than music'. Occasionally a more frivolous subject was debated, such as 'A little knowledge is not a dangerous thing'. The results of some debates showed a narrow and conservative ethos: it was agreed that 'Women should be withheld from voting in elections for Parliament', that women should not be admitted to degrees in literature and science, and 'That the sooner the Welsh language dies out the better' (this from an institution located in a Welsh-speaking part of Britain). The motion 'That the state does well in compelling parents to educate their children' was defeated. Hopkins spoke in favour of Welsh, the practice of keeping a diary, and, ironically, that 'A theological student should eschew all literature not bearing on his studies' (*HTJ*, 159-60, 246-56).

In this, Hopkins was conforming with a recent complaint received from the Superior General of the Jesuits, that the St Beuno's students spent too much time on light reading. The Beadle's journal for 28 January 1877 reads:

> Rev. Fr. Rector ... wished all to consult a Professor or Superior ... on the advisability of reading this or that author or book, then fortified with the sanction of one of the above Revd Fathers to obtain the minister's leave to take the book out of the Library.
> (*HTJ*, 172)

This example of narrowness and fear of unsanctioned stimulation of intellect or senses was one of many. The same journal entry records: 'His reverence drew attention to the rule of silence and of speaking Latin. It was not necessary to obtain leave to visit another provided the business transacted came under "obiter et perpaucis" [in passing, and in very few words]. Beyond this leave was necessary.' At another date there is the entry: 'F. Rector objects to the scholastics walking in the garden after dark'.

There was also an essay society, or Academy, on Saturday nights, again with a narrow-angled list of subjects: 'The power of the Church to grant indulgences', 'Early history of the Vulgate', 'Ballerini's view on usury', 'St Cyprian on the unity of the Church', and 'St Augustine's *City of God*'. Hopkins contributed a paper on 'The composition of place in the Spiritual Exercises' (*HTJ*, 173).

One constant discomfort for a large part of the year was the inadequate heating. In his first letter home from St Beuno's Hopkins wrote that 'pipes of affliction convey lukewarm water of affliction to some of the rooms, others more fortunate have fires' (*L3*, 124). But fires were allowed only from mid-October to mid-April; one hopes that a touch of commonsense and humanity was shown in 1876, when the Beadle's log read: 'April 11. Great fall of snow last night; April 12. Heavy fall of snow; April 17. Cold East wind' (*HTJ*, 167). A year earlier Hopkins had written on 24 April: 'Such a backward spring I cannot remember ... our climate on the hillside is a touch Arctic' (*L3*, 132). The Minister's log contains several entries about the chronic cold and damp. In February 1877, one of the scholastics was attacked

> by a rush of blood to the head. Dr says this resulted from excessive cold to which occupying a room in [the] western front in the attic story he is necessarily subject. The pipes were as hot as possible but could not contend against the continual currents of cold air rushing in thro chinks in doors, windows, walls and floors.
> (*HTJ*, 175-6)

In his first two years Hopkins suffered from indigestion and colds. There is no record of anything worse, but he was not allowed to fast during Lent more often than once a week, and was sometimes sent out for a ride in the trap, a treat reserved for those in bad health. In his third year he again had colds and also wrote 'I am thinner, I think, than ever I was before now' (*L3*, 146). Several times he was sent to Rhyl 'for the good of his health', although, as the poem 'The Sea and the Skylark' shows, that 'frail and shallow' town was anathema to him.

Besides the cold the community had to put up with an inadequate water supply, which meant that a bath could be taken 'not oftener than once a month'. Not surprisingly Hopkins developed piles, which were to cause him constant trouble in the future, and for a painful fortnight just before he finally left St Beuno's, at the end of his third year there, was confined to bed and was operated on for circumcision.

Hopkins fell prey to a mild hypochondria, so that, increasingly, he would complain of strange and sometimes unconvincing ailments, symptoms of mental unease rather than physical. His stay at St Beuno's is characterised by frequent manifestations of his desire for live, natural, human, spontaneous, interesting objects and occurrences – 'All things counter, original, spare, strange', as he expressed it – emphases repressed and discouraged by the crippling, humdrum and repetitive, daily regime he forced himself to suffer.

At St Beuno's, for the first time in his life bar the failure to gain the 1862 Balliol scholarship, Hopkins did badly in examinations. He passed the first-year examinations in moral theology and dogma, but only just, three of his four examiners giving him a third-class grade, and the other a fourth. He also passed at the end of his second year, as well as the test in March of his third year 'ad audiendas confessiones', but on 22 July 1877 failed the most important examination. Needing three positive votes from the four examiners, he received only two, both awarding him only a low pass. Ten of his classmates were allowed to enter the important fourth year of theological study, but not Hopkins. This meant that Hopkins never attained the grade of a professed father in the Society, only the lower degree of a 'spiritual coadjutor'. From the start of his Jesuit career it had been assumed by everyone, including Hopkins, that his progress would be smooth and straightforward. Then had come the sudden shock of this failure, having to say goodbye to his fellow students and companions of the last three or more years, and, above all, being forced by his own inability to absorb and conform to the rules to leave his beloved Wild Wales, a Mother of Muses to him, breathing poetry.

Jesuit writers on Hopkins have sometimes been guilty of preferring their ideal preconceptions of Hopkins to the evidence. Fr Lahey, for instance, having admitted that Hopkins's 'avocation for Scotism eventually became a passion with him ... so that he was often embroiled in minor duels of intellect', concludes, in the first biography of Hopkins, that 'he completed a successful course of theology at St Beuno's and left there with the reputation of being one of the best moral theologians among his contemporaries' (*Lahey*, 132). And Fr Thomas, while conceding that 'his penchant for the opinions of Duns Scotus may have served to bar him from a fourth year of study', lays emphasis on a cause for which Hopkins could not be blamed, 'the dubious state of his health' (*HTJ*, 182).

These accounts devalue or overlook vital pieces of evidence about Hopkins's true theological tastes. In August 1872, when he was a second-year philosopher at Stonyhurst, Hopkins had noted: 'At this time I had first begun to get hold of the copy of Scotus on the Sentences ... and was flush with a new stroke of enthusiasm ... just then when I took in any inscape of the sky or sea I thought of Scotus' (*J*, 221). And at St Beuno's, in spite of his support for the motion that a theological student 'should eschew all literature not bearing on his studies', Hopkins had written to Bridges: 'After all I can, at all events a little, read Duns Scotus and I care for him more even than Aristotle' (L1, 31). Joseph Rickaby, a contemporary of Hopkins's, wrote that 'in speculative theology [Hopkins] was a strong Scotist, and read Scotus assiduously. That led to his being plucked at the end of his third year: he was too Scotist for his examiners' (Farm Street, Lahey Papers). And Jesuits who had known him during his last days in Ireland recorded:

> as a theologian his undoubted brilliance was dimmed by a somewhat obstinate love of Scotist doctrine, in which he traced the influences of Platonist philosophy. His idiosyncrasy got him into difficulties with his Jesuit preceptors who followed Aquinas and Aristotle. The strain of controversy added to bad health had marred his earlier years.
> (HTJ, 183)

Hopkins instinctively agreed with Scotus's objection to Aristotle's and Aquinas's emphasis on the intellect as final judge; as Devlin puts it: 'To put final felicity in the intellect is to abandon man's noblest gift, his freedom; for the intellect has no choice' (S, 346). Scotus also allowed the senses a larger and more important role than did the official theologians, who were frightened by them; in several poems Hopkins wrote in Wales he assigns values to the senses which would be quite foreign to his official studies. Hopkins's last reference to Scotus, in a letter written several years after he had left St Beuno's, reveals a rueful personal identification with the discarded and undervalued philosopher:

> And so I used to feel of Duns Scotus when I used to read him with delight: he saw too far, he knew too much; his subtlety overshot his interests; a kind of feud arose between genius and talent, and the ruck of talent in the Schools finding itself, as his age passed by, less and less able to understand him, voted that there was nothing important to understand.
> (L3, 349)

Because of the rejection of his views in the theology examination and in the negative judgement on his great poem 'The Wreck of the Deutschland', Hopkins's confidence in himself as a Jesuit and as a poet suffered greatly. From now onwards, he seemed increasingly a lone figure, the outsider, prone to dark melancholy, assigned a constant round of unsettled posts, with no sense of permanence. The poetry he wrote after he left Wales became more self-absorbed, with little or no sense of an audience either in the present or in the forseeable future. But at least 'The Wreck of the Deutschland' had been written. That occurred in Hopkins's second year at St Beuno's in the winter of 1875-1876.

Six
'A shipping disaster is a godsend':
'The Wreck of the Deutschland'

Dominated geographically by the surrounding seas and oceans, with no spot further than seventy miles from the coast, Victorian Britain was essentially a maritime power. People were conscious of their dependency on the sea to maintain the nation's dominance in trade and military ascendancy. The perennial characterisation of the British as the Island race with salt in their blood, gallantly defending themselves in their tiny ships against more powerful foreigners, was constantly chronicled in fictional reconstructions of Elizabethan and Napoleonic battles. Many non-sea-going Victorians developed a nautical vocabulary.

It could be patriotic merely to depict the sea. Turner's paintings of terrifying tempests, boatloads of the shipwrecked, blazing sunsets at sea, and steamers in snow-storms, appeared to have universal significance, while poets such as Matthew Arnold found that the sea symbolised the solitariness of an individual's struggle against the vast and uncontrollable impersonality of the age:

A God, a God their severance ruled!
And bade betwixt their shore to be
The unplumb'd, salt, estranging sea.
('To Marguerite', 22-24)

Disasters were headlined in newspapers, and there was an eager market for reports and illustrations which gave all the horrific human details; there was even a popular parlour-game called 'Railway Accidents', where the players simulated 'two engines

91

crashed together in a horrible collision'. The Victorians were not squeamish about death, and sometimes their comfortable armchair savouring of human suffering approaches the pornographic. The restrained emotion of Whiting's hymn, 'O hear us when we cry to Thee / For those in peril on the sea', has to be set against numerous poems which exploited popular melodramatic sentiments about shipwrecks: 'Down the deep sea, full fourscore fathoms down, / An iron vault hath clutched five hundred men!'

*　*　*

One of the few newspapers that were available in the recreation room at St Beuno's was *The Times*, and for five days in early December 1875 its issues were read with unusual and growing excitement by Brother Gerard Hopkins. On Wednesday 8 December, on page five *The Times* printed three telegrams and a Press Association report which together gave a vivid picture of how news of a dreadful shipwreck in the mouth of the Thames had reached first Sheerness, then Lloyd's in London, then Harwich, and then the press.

At about noon on the previous day a small lifeboat had come ashore at Sheerness carrying one living man and two dead. The boat had put out thirty-eight hours before from a steamer which had struck a sandbank in the North Sea; the survivor, the ship's quarter-master, called August Beck, said that the crew and passengers together numbered a hundred and fifty, and he thought that all the rest had been lost.

The Harwich correspondent of *The Times* quickly collected together pieces of shipping information from Lloyd's, the port authorities, the passenger lists, and Mr O.J. Williams, the North German consul at Harwich, and telegraphed the resulting picture to his paper:

> The North German Lloyd steamer *Deutschland*, of Bremen, Captain Brickenstein, from Bremen for New York, with emigrants, grounded on the Kentish Knock [south-east of Harwich, north-north-east of Margate] on Monday morning during a gale from the north-east, thick with snow.

The Harwich tug, the *Liverpool*, he said, had landed some of the crew and passengers, though it was thought that about fifty had been drowned. Thirteen of the twenty-six cabin passengers were listed as missing: 'Ludwig Heerman, J. Grossman, Maria Forster, Emil Hack, Bertha Fundling, Theodor Fundling, five nuns [who were among the second-class passengers], Procopi Kadolkoff, and O. Lundgren'; the ninety-seven between-decks steerage passengers were not mentioned. 'Missing' was probably an inaccuracy as, *The Times* reported two days later, the *Liverpool* had brought thirteen bodies to Harwich. That Tuesday evening, Quartermaster Beck, though still sleepless and suffering greatly from exposure, had recovered sufficiently to make a personal statement. He described how, having left Bremen on the Saturday, the *Deutschland* encountered a regular gale on Sunday morning, and that evening, 'during a storm, we struck on a [sand]bank and stuck fast':

> It had been blowing heavily. We tried to get off, but could not; the sea washed over us fore and aft, carrying away much of our gear. The captain kept very cool, and when the vessel grounded he ordered the lifebelts to be served out to both the passengers and crew.

Thinking the ship was about to break up, the quartermaster and two seamen got into one lifeboat, found themselves adrift, and could make no 'head against the heavy sea'.

> The last I saw of the ship they were endeavouring to launch all the boats. The sea was very wild at the time, and the ship laboured heavily. I got up a small sail, and drifted before the wind, but my two mates were soon helpless through the blinding snow and piercing cold. One died the same night and the other on the next morning. On Monday I saw several ships and made signs of distress, but none came near me. On Tuesday I passed a lightship and called out again, but I suppose they did not hear me. I saw a light on shore, and luckily managed to steer my boat to it.

The quartermaster was too exhausted to give further details, but added 'I hope to have a better night's sleep to-night than I have had these last three nights.'

The Times the following morning, Thursday 9 December, carried a much longer and more ordered report, on page six. The North German Lloyd Company had issued a statement emphasising the perfect safety record of their line, the generous provision of lifeboats and life-belts on the *Deutschland*, the many years experience of her master and purser, and the fact that there had been both a Weser pilot and an English Channel pilot on board when she struck. (Later it emerged that there was also a third pilot on board.) A reporter had found details of the ship's size, tonnage, engine-power, and construction in the 'Liverpool Underwriters' Book of Iron Vessels'; though not registered at Lloyd's, she was of British build, having been launched on the Clyde in 1866.

The first precise account of the wreck-scene was given by a crew-member:

> The steamer struck on Monday morning at 5 o'clock. The sea was very rough, blowing hard from the east-north-east, thick with snow. The lead was cast every half-hour. We found 24 fathoms and then 17 fathoms. Immediately afterwards she struck, ship going dead slow. The engines were turned full speed astern, and immediately lost propellor. The ship was then driven further up [on the sandbank].

Two boats were then lowered, but as both filled with water, the sea appeared too rough to launch more, and eventually the rest of the boats were washed overboard. Cargo was thrown overboard in an attempt to keep part of the ship afloat, and passengers sheltered in the deck-houses. The pumps were kept going the whole day, but as dusk came the tide rose, the decks became awash, and passengers and crew compelled to take to the rigging. Captain Brickenstein remained on the bridge until forced to join the others on the rigging. The tug Liverpool had arrived about noon on Tuesday, thirty-one hours after the steamer had struck the sandbank.

The vital question was asked why the ship had deviated from her course to ground on the shifting sands of the Kentish Knock, and a possible answer put forward: 'As the wind was blowing strongly from the east-north-east it is perhaps a reasonable presumption that the numerous shoals of the Dutch coast were sought to be avoided by a westerly course, with the result that the ship approached too close to the Thames shoals'.

The next day's, Friday's, paper carried on page ten a long account of the inquest at Harwich on the thirteen bodies brought ashore by the *Liverpool*. It went into a lot of detail, the chief witnesses' accounts having been taken down in shorthand and printed verbatim. The appalling weather conditions, of a heavy gale and snow-storm, so that six look-out men were of little use, the frequent casting of the lead, the sudden sight of breakers, the breaking of the screw, so that the ship was at the mercy of wind and waves, the striking on the sands, the firing of the rockets – all were the staple ingredients of sea-disasters both in reality and in poems such as Longfellow's 'The Wreck of the Hesperus'.

The business of Hopkins's father Manley as an average adjuster was in the main to allocate to each underwriter of a shipping claim in the case of a wreck the proportion relating to his particular insurance. (The adjustment could take several years to compile and fees sometimes ran to over a thousand pounds.) And the question of marine insurance had already cropped up in the newspaper reports, as the shipping company were 'their own insurers', and so responsible for all the losses. But Gerard Hopkins had never shown the slightest interest in his father's work, leaving the task of carrying on the family business to his next younger brother Cyril. So it is unlikely that Hopkins's interest was aroused until the first graphic details of the human plight, and especially that of the five German nuns, were recorded on page seven of *The Times* that Saturday morning.

The report started: 'The bodies of the four German nuns were removed today for interment at a convent of the Franciscan order, to which they belonged, near Stratford.' Although Stratford was Hopkins's birthplace, it was not this that aroused his interest. It was the dramatic account at the end of the report of the height of the horror that caught his eye and heart:

> At 2 a.m., Captain Brickenstein, knowing that with the rising tide the ship would be waterlogged, ordered all the passengers to come on deck. Danger levels class distinctions, and steerage and first-class passengers were by this time together in the after saloon and cabins. Most of them obeyed the summons at once; others lingered below till it was too late; some of the ill, weak, despairing of life even on deck, resolved to stay in their cabins and meet death without any further struggle to evade it. After 3

95

a.m. on Tuesday morning a scene of horror was witnessed. Some passengers clustered for safety within or upon the wheelhouse, and on the top of other slight structures on deck. Most of the crew and many of the emigrants went into the rigging, where they were safe enough as long as they could maintain their hold. But the intense cold and long exposure told a tale. The purser of the ship, though a strong man, relaxed his grasp, and fell into the sea. Women and children and men were one by one swept away from their shelters on the deck. Five German nuns, whose bodies are now in the dead-house here, clasped hands and were drowned together, the chief sister, a gaunt woman 6 ft. high, calling out loudly and often 'O Christ, come quickly!' till the end came. The shrieks and sobbing of women and children are described by the survivors as agonizing. One brave sailor, who was safe in the rigging, went down to try and save a child or woman who was drowning on deck. He was secured by a rope to the rigging, but a wave dashed him against the bulwarks, and when daylight dawned his headless body, detained by the rope, was swaying to and fro with the waves. In the dreadful excitement of these hours one man hung himself behind the wheelhouse, another hacked at his wrist with a knife, hoping to die a comparatively painless death by bleeding. It was nearly 8 o'clock before the tide abated, and the survivors could venture to go on deck. At half-past 10 o'clock the tugboat from Harwich came alongside and brought all away without further accident.

On the following Monday morning *The Times* carried three separate articles on the *Deutschland* disaster, plus letters from the Mayor of Harwich and Lord Strafford (who offered to provide Harwich with a lifeboat) in the correspondence columns, showing the now widespread national interest. On page nine there was a long and indignant attack on the Mayor of Harwich for his 'inadequate excuses' for the lack of a lifeboat, and for the behaviour of those inhabitants of his town who had left the *Deutschland* 'to her fate during a long winter's night and dismal morning'. People all over Britain would be shocked to learn 'that a wreck could be stranded off the English coast, appealing to English sailors for aid, and for thirty hours should be left without that aid', although 'the signals of distress were seen and recognized by the Harwich seamen'.

The article went on, in a strong piece of hostile investigative-journalism, to contrast the Mayor's demands for public gratitude for

1. St Beuno's: 'a medley of ricks and dovecots'

2. The Vale of Clwyd

3 & 4. Friends of Hopkins's at St Beuno's: Henry Schomber Kerr SJ and Francis Bacon SJ

5. St Beuno's gardens: the centre walk

6. St Beuno's: the tower

7. The Caerwys woods

8 & 9. Teachers at St Beuno's: Frs Peter Gallwey SJ and John Morris SJ

10. Ffynnon Fair (Mary's Well)

11. Ffynnon Fair

13. The Tombstone

12. St Winefride's Well

14. The
Wreck of the
Deutschland

Harwich seamen who, in the words of his letter, 'have been saving materials and cargo from the ship', with the true picture of a crowd of 'salvors' who 'descended upon the helpless steamer and revelled in pillage', even rifling possessions from bodies of the drowned, though the owner's agents had already boarded the ship 'and given notice that she was not derelict'.

In column 1 of the following page there was a vivid description of the pillagers at work:

> The owner's agent and the third mate of the *Deutschland* went aboard on Wednesday, and found 50 or 60 men at work in the cabins and on deck, breaking open passengers' luggage, fishing cargo up out of the hold, stripping the saloon and cabins – in short, wrecking the ship. It was in vain that the mate and the owners' representative interposed and warned them off. The work of pillage – it can hardly be called by any other name – went on, and on Thursday ... the wreckers had left little in the saloon and cabins worth carrying off, and had stripped the ship of braces, running gear, rigging, leaving, in fact, 'hardly a rope yarn'. I wish this were the worst that had to be told. Twenty bodies have now been brought into Harwich by the steamtug. Mr. Guy, the inspector of police here, tells me that, with one exception, not a single valuable was found on the persons of these unfortunate people, and that it was clear their pockets had been turned out and rifled. There were ring-marks on the fingers of women, and of at least one gentleman. The rings themselves had disappeared. One poor fellow wore a second pair of trousers, and in a pocket of the inside pair there was a thaler and two smaller pieces of silver.

The fourteen smacks and luggers that were gathered round the wreck came from 'the fishing village in the Colne river and from Whitstable, Ramsgate, and Margate'. The article concluded with information about the legal position on 'valuable and portable salvage', and suggestions as to how such disgraceful scenes could have been avoided.

The details, description, and arguments thus far would have provided Manley Hopkins, the poet's father, with plenty of material and interest to exercise his well-oiled talents at verse-writing: it would be fascinating to compare the father's account with his son's.

What caught and held Gerard's attention was the third article on the wreck in that day's *Times*, in the adjacent column on page ten:

Four of the five nuns who perished by the wreck are to be buried at Leytonstone today. They belonged to a Franciscan nunnery in Westphalia, and are regarded by their co-religionists in London as having been exiled from their native land in consequence of Falck Laws. When their deaths became known it was resolved by the authorities of the Roman Catholic Church in London to give the bodies solemn burial. For this purpose two Franciscan fathers were despatched to Harwich, and the bodies were placed in oak coffins lined with white satin, and brought to London on Friday evening. On reaching Stratford they were delivered over to the care of the nuns at the Convent of Jesus and Mary, who assisted by the nuns of the Sacred Heart, prepared their dead sisters for burial. The dead nuns were wearing, with slight variation, the dress common to the order; and as there was found on each dress the number assigned to a nun in making her profession of religion, all will, no doubt, in this way be identified. After being made ready the bodies lay in state in the spacious classroom below the Franciscan church at Stratford throughout Saturday and yesterday. The open coffins lay side by side upon a raised dais, lighted candles were placed beside the coffins, while vases of flowers and wreaths of immortelles were grouped at the heads and feet. Upon both days large numbers of people visited the place, the major portion of whom appeared to be prompted by feelings of devotion. The deceased appeared to be between the ages of thirty and forty, and their faces wore an expression of calmness and resignation. Their fingers were clasped upon a rosary and crucifix; upon the breast of each lay a cross of white flowers, the gifts of the Ursuline nuns of Upton. One, noted for her extreme tallness, is the lady who, at midnight on Monday, by standing on a table in the saloon, was able to thrust her body through the skylight, and kept exclaiming in a voice heard by those in the rigging above the roar of the storm, 'My God, my God, make haste, make haste'. There will be a solemn mass (*coram archiepiscopo*) in the Franciscan church, Stratford, this morning at 11. Cardinal Manning will deliver a funeral oration over the deceased, after which they will be interred in St. Patrick's Catholic Cemetery, Leytonstone.

Subsequently Hopkins must have read in *The Times* much more about the wreck of the *Deutschland*; there were unsettled issues – not least about who was to blame for the grounding of the ship on the Kentish Knock – with many further reports on Coroners' and Inquiry courts, and several column inches of correspondence. The official inquiry was held a fortnight after the disaster, and Inspector Rothery's report published at the end of February 1876, though *The Times* had printed a brief abstract of it three weeks earlier. The inquiry concluded that

> The master ought, from the warnings he received, to have known that his ship was out of her position, and knowing this, it would have been his duty to have put her about ... and returned slowly upon his course. For not doing so, we think he was greatly to blame.

The disaster was 'due to the vessel having got ahead of her reckoning, owing to the disregard by the master of the force and direction of the tide'. From the moment when the vessel struck, however, Captain Brickenstein's conduct had been exemplary.

All the factual details of the event that Hopkins needed for his poem were contained in the first five days' reports in *The Times* already referred to. He would almost certainly have seen the three vivid sketches in *The Illustrated London News*, subscribed to by the college, of pillaging by the local fishermen, 'Wreck of the Deutschland as it appeared in the morning of Thursday week', and 'Rescue of the Survivors of the Deutschland by the Harwich Steam-Tug Liverpool', but considered them irrelevant to the poem, and he would have read in *The Tablet* Cardinal Manning's sermon delivered at the Requiem for the *Deutschland* sisters. This was composed in 'Bishops' prose' (as a Jesuit priest recently described it to me), and gave a pious but doubtful interpretation of the nuns' refusal to obey the ship's captain's order to come on deck:

> These good Sisters were so resigned in the tranquillity of their confidence in God, that they showed not the smallest sign of agitation or fear. They remained quietly in their cabin, and at length when they were asked to mount the riggings, as a last chance of safety, they refused – they were already prepared for the great voyage of eternity – life and death were the same to them. When at length a means of escape was at hand they allowed others to take their places and to save themselves. Can you imagine the

horror of their position during the anxious hours of waiting [?] What terrible scenes about them. The agony, the despair, the piercing cries of their fellow passengers. The roaring of the tempest, the terrifying cracking of the vessel; and nevertheless in such surroundings a divine calm pacified the souls of these holy victims.... Powerful indeed must have been their example. And like an eloquent voice it surely strengthened the courage of others like themselves who were soon to be there no longer.

(Stratford Reference Library)

Dr Leo van Noppen, author of the most thorough and authoritative study of the poem, tells me:

The discrepancy between Cardinal Manning's observations on the exemplary behaviour of the nuns in the early hours of 7 December 1875 and all the published (eyewitness) accounts of the same episode is remarkable indeed. In all my researches ... I have not come across a single shred of evidence for Card. Manning's claims that the nuns 'showed not the smallest sign of agitation or fear' or that 'they allowed others to take their places' in the rigging. On the contrary, reports in *The Daily News* (9 Dec), *Nieuwe Amsterdamsche Courant* (11 Dec), *The East Kent Mercury* (18 Dec), and *The New York Herald* (27 Dec) not only corroborate the facts mentioned in *The Times* and the Enquiry Report, but do so in greater and more dramatic detail. To their fellow-passengers it certainly looked as if the nuns were scared to death and in a state of uncontrollable panic (see e.g. the account in *The Daily News*).

The eyewitness account in The Daily News for 9 December 1875 reads:

There were five nuns on board who, by their terror-stricken conduct, seem to have added greatly to the weirdness of the scene. They were deaf to all entreaties to leave the saloon, and when, almost by main force, the stewardess (whose conduct throughout was plucky in the extreme) managed to get them on to the companion ladder, they sank down on the steps and stubbornly refused to go another step. They seemed to have returned to the saloon again shortly, for somewhere in the dead of the night, when the greater part of the crew and passengers were in the rigging, one was seen with her body half through the skylight, crying aloud in a voice heard above the storm, 'O, my God, make it

quick! make it quick!'... A man tied to the mast nearer the deck
had his head cut off by the waves, as Herrmann [one of the pas-
sengers] says, though probably a rope or a loose spar was the
agent. Not far off, a little boy had his leg broken in the same
manner. They could hear and see a nun shrieking through the
skylight, and when she was silenced the cry was taken up by a
woman wailing from the wheelhouse, 'My child is drowned, my
little one, Adam'.... Five Roman Catholic nuns from Paderborn
were among the women; they prayed aloud that God would
send them a speedy death, and so end their misery. ('Ach Gott!
mache es nur kurz, wenn wir schon sterben müssen!').
(*LvN*, 19)

Hopkins probably was ignorant of the *Daily News* version of events,
because of the very restricted range of papers and journals at St
Beuno's, and his limited contact with the world outside. He must
have rejected Manning's interpretation through a mixture of enthusiasm for his own strong emotions and perception of a hidden deeper
shape in the events of the wreck, and lack of sympathy for the official unctuousness of the Requiem sermon. Although Hopkins had
been confirmed as a Roman Catholic by Manning, it was a very different type of Catholic, John Henry Newman, who had received him
into the church in October 1866; and whereas Hopkins and Newman
remained in contact until Hopkins's death, Hopkins had no
recorded friendship or even sympathy with Manning.

Blake Morrison has coherently proposed that Hopkins's reactions to the fate of the nuns was closely tied up with his roots in
Stratford, asking the question: 'Did Hopkins know that the four
nuns had been laid out [in the hall under St Francis' church] almost
opposite 87 The Grove [Hopkins's birthplace], and was that part of
the reason the tragedy moved him to write poetry again after a
period of silence?' And Morrison ingeniously suggests that the
phrase 'at our door / Drowned', in the final stanza, 'could be a
reference not just to England in general but, more slyly, to the nuns
at the door of his old house' (*Independent on Sunday*, 24 July 1994).
The grand patriotic theme at the end of the poem is both so strong
and so formally controlled that I doubt Hopkins would allow himself such a deviant and petty personal indulgence. Hopkins's
Dominical sermon on 'Make the men sit down', which I have

mentioned as containing fussy digressions, was much more casually composed.

There was more press coverage over this shipwreck than over any other for some time before and after the event, and several stories peripherally connected arose afterwards, such as that of the nineteen-year-old girl, Mary Broadway, who worked in Tillett's Laundry in Stratford:

> Mary rose to the occasion. She borrowed some sheets to wrap the bodies in while she took the sodden habits to wash and dry. Having accomplished this, she laid the nuns out in their clean, dry habits, with their written vows, which she had found in little bags round their necks, placed in their joined hands.... In 1880 when Mary was 23 she entered the Franciscan Convent at Woodchester in Gloucestershire.
> (Stratford Reference Library)

This was probably how it was discovered that the fifth nun, whose body had not been found, was Sr Henrica Fassbender, aged twenty-eight, who on the morning of her departure for America, had left in the cell of her Superior, Mother Clara, a poem, 'Farewell', which included these two stanzas (presumably originally in German):

> Now the solemn hour of departure is at hand,
> And my heart, deeply touched, throbs with fear;
> 'Tis bleeding as though pierced by many a spear,
> For in bitter pain we leave you and our land so dear.
>
> Yes, bless me, Mother! God can and will heed
> The prayerful blessing your fingers trace on me;
> I need not fear – God knows best my every need –
> Is he not ruler over land and sea?
> (Stratford Reference Library)

Hopkins probably did not know this poem, though the finger image is similar to that in the first stanza of Hopkins's ode.

(On 13 December a huge crowd joined the funeral procession of cross-bearer, over fifty priests, nuns from a nearby convent, Catholic school-children, and the four hearses, to St Patrick's cemetery,

Leytonstone, where the bodies were buried in plot A.13, grave 373. Hopkins did not attend. A headstone, inscribed with fanciful and stylish lettering, was added some time later, when the names had been confirmed, and a further, plainer inscription chiselled on the front kerbstone in 1978.)

* * *

Hopkins 'was affected by the account and happening to say so to my rector he said that he wished someone would write a poem on the subject. On this hint I set to work and, though my hand was out at first, produced one' (*L2*, 14). I'm afraid I don't give much credence to the idea that Hopkins took up someone else's suggestion to write the poem. As often happens to creative people Hopkins managed to find opportunities to exercise his gifts when his muse urged; with him there would have to be a plausible alternative, a sanction from outside his control, which he could persuade his conscience was the prime mover, and somehow his rector played this part sufficiently well for Hopkins to release himself from his vow of poetic silence made on becoming a Jesuit – 'to write no more, as not belonging to my profession'.

Unable to rely on obtaining the college copies of *The Times* he asked his mother to send relevant parts of the Oak Hill ones, but she missed some and duplicated another. By Christmas Eve he had not only started writing the poem but was also considering where it would be published.

In the next chapter I will discuss ways in which Hopkins gained inspiration from the Welsh language for his poetry, even though his knowledge of it was sparse and imperfect, and its usage by him subjective and unscholarly. There were other partially dormant linguistic and poetic skills waiting for the opportunity to joyfully emerge. From his early writings onwards, taught by Ruskin's example, Hopkins had been vitally interested in capturing in words the visual look and impact of water. It had been in the journal of his 1868 Swiss holiday that he had first given extended accounts of water behaviour in descriptions of falls, streams, glaciers, and lakes:

Then we saw the three falls of the Reichenbach. The upper one is the biggest. At the take-off it falls in discharges of rice or meal but each cluster as it descends sharpens and tapers, and from halfway down the whole cascade is inscaped in fretted falling vandykes in each of which the frets or points, just like the startings of a just-lit lucifer match, keep shooting in races, one beyond the other, to the bottom. The vapour which beats up from the impact of the falling water makes little feeder rills down the rocks and these catching and running in drops along the sharp ledges in the rock are shaken and delayed and chased along them and even cut off and blown upwards by the blast of the vapour as it rises.

(J, 177)

This had been followed in 1870 by an exuberant description of the river Hodder, near Stonyhurst:

Yesterday [the river] was a sallow glassy gold at Hodder Roughs and by watching hard the banks began to sail upstream, the scaping unfolded, the river was all in tumult but not running, only the lateral motions were perceived, and the curls of froth where the waves overlap shaped and turned easily and idly.... Today the river was wild, very full, glossy brown with mud, furrowed in permanent billows, through which from head to head the water swung with a great down and up again. These heads were scalped with jags of jumping foam. But at the Roughs the sight was the hurly water-backs which heave after heave kept tumbling up from the broken foam and their plump heap turning open in ropes of velvet.

(J, 200)

And on an Isle of Man holiday in 1872 Hopkins had become fluent at verbalising seascapes, achieving remarkable graphic and evocative power. Walking on the Manx cliffs he had discovered a new challenge, namely to conjure adequate verbal equivalents of fleeting pieces of sea in action:

First, say, it is an install of green marble knotted with ragged white, then fields of white lather, the comb of the wave richly clustered and crisped in breaking, then it is broken small and so unfolding till it runs in threads and thrums twitching down the backdraught to the sea again.

(J, 225)

The sometimes arcane vocabulary and syntax he had simultaneously developed encouraged the feeling that he was secretly visiting the penetralia of some deity of the physical universe. It was not
just a gift for sea description and metaphor he had developed but
also an appetite which needed food; the sea's variety gave him the
greatest challenge and opportunities for combining verbal inven-
tiveness with closely accurate observation. Also, he had always felt
strongly attracted to nature in excess: violent nature provoked in
him potent emotional responses and a verbal vitality extraordinary
in its originality.

To many readers, including me, the most successful and moving
part of the poem is the account of the ship in the storm, where
Hopkins uses details from the reports in *The Times*, sometimes the
exact words (stanzas 13 to 17). Here the current of meaning keeps
flowing unhesitatingly and very strongly, without the plot or vocabulary or imagery becoming incomprehensible to the reader:

> Into the snows she sweeps,
>   Hurling the haven behind,
> The Deutschland, on Sunday; and so the sky keeps,
>   For the infinite air is unkind,
> And the sea flint-flake, black-backed in the regular blow,
> Sitting Eastnortheast, in cursed quarter, the wind;
>   Wiry and white-fiery and whirlwind-swivelled snow
> Spins to the widow-making unchilding unfathering deeps.
>
>   She drove in the dark to leeward,
>   She struck — not a reef or a rock
> But the combs of a smother of sand: night drew her
>   Dead to the Kentish Knock;
> And she beat the bank down with her bows and the ride of her keel;
> The breakers rolled on her beam with ruinous shock;
>   And canvass and compass, the whorl and the wheel
> Idle for ever to waft her or wind her with, these she endured.
>
>   Hope had grown grey hairs,
>   Hope had mourning on,
> Trenched with tears, carved with cares,
>   Hope was twelve hours gone;
> And frightful a nightfall folded rueful a day
> Nor rescue, only rocket and lightship, shone,

And lives at last were washing away:
To the shrouds they took, – they shook in the hurling and horrible airs.

One stirred from the rigging to save
The wild woman-kind below,
With a rope's end round the man, hardy and brave –
He was pitched to his death at a blow,
For all his dreadnought breast and braids of thew:
They could tell him for hours, dandled the to and fro
Through the cobbled foam-fleece. What could he do
With the burl of the fountains of air, buck and flood of the wave?

They fought with God's cold –
And they could not and fell to the deck
(Crushed them) or water (and drowned them) or rolled
With the sea-romp over the wreck.
Night roared, with the heart-break hearing a heart-broke rabble,
The woman's wailing, the crying of child without check –
Till a lioness arose breasting the babble,
A prophetess towered in the tumult, a virginal tongue told.

As well as by accepting his rector's suggestion as sanction, Hopkins could have overcome his scruples against poetry-writing by recalling Plato's advocacy of poetic types which educated, and past examples of the Pindaric ode, whose form Hopkins adapted for his poem, showed how capable it was of serving such a didactic purpose. To Hopkins this shipwreck did not appear – as it would have done to many of his contemporaries – merely another depressing example of the power of cosmic determinism and the absence of an ordinary Providence. Pindar's odes frequently elevated ordinary events to ones of universal significance, and in a similar way Hopkins passionately wanted his poem to show, by identifying the nature and significance of the nun's action, that the wreck was the antithesis of the shapeless and the accidental.

Hopkins's poem has the ostensible aim of religious poetry, 'to animate devotion' (in Dr Johnson's words); but as Johnson says, devotional poetry seldom attains this end:

The essence of poetry is invention; such invention as, by producing something unexpected, surprises and delights. The topics of devotion are few, and being few are universally known;

but, few as there are, they can be made no more; they can receive
no grace from novelty of sentiment, and very little from novelty
of expression.

Most readers, I think, find great difficulty in grasping the poem
as a whole. The narrative structure of those parts of Hopkins's poem
which deal with his religious interpretation of the event is particularly unclear, even if the reader (or listener) is in sympathy with the
religious doctrines and mental habits the poet assumes. It is also
necessary for the reader to agree with the poet's interpretations of
coincidences, which are sometimes incredible and naive rather than
finely inventive discoveries.

The greatness of 'The Wreck of the Deutschland', I think, does
not depend on its religious arguments, which often hamper the
poetry. In fact, from the vital climax of the argument, the heroine's
cry 'O Christ, Christ, come quickly' in stanza 24, onwards, the poem
seems in large parts to become bogged down in, at times, clumsily
worded and versified, unclear religious argument. Almost every
one of the final eleven stanzas has at least one stumbling line which
spoils nearby graceful or powerful ones, and prevents there being
any examples of unarguably felicitous complete stanzas, such as frequently occur in the first twenty stanzas:

They were else-minded, altogether, the men (25)

The treasure never eyesight got, nor was ever guessed what for
the hearing? (26)

Wording it how but by him that present and past,
Heaven and earth are word of, worded by? (29)

For so conceived, so to conceive thee is done; (30)

the breast of the
Maiden could obey so, be a bell to, ring of it, and (31)

Hopkins seems in the last part of the poem to have experienced
much more difficulty in expressing his meaning within the longer
lines (5 to 8) of the stanza form than he did at first.

The extent to which one is convinced by the main argument

depends largely on the poet's interpretation of the nun's words 'O Christ, come quickly!' or 'O, my God, make it quick! make it quick!' which, as Van Noppen says, her fellow-passengers assumed to indicate that they were 'scared to death and in a state of uncontrollable panic'. In stanza 28 the rather feeble solution to the question 'what did she mean?' is given: Christ 'was to cure the extremity where he had cast her'; this in the stanza which much more cleverly imitates in verse the mental process of the poet as he realises the significance of the nun's cry:

> But how shall I ... make me room there:
> Reach me a ... Fancy, come faster –
> Strike you the sight of it? look at it loom there,
> Thing that she ... There, then! the Master.

What provokes most of the many undoubted successes in the poem is personal direct experience, related with such vivid immediacy that the activity seems to be taking place simultaneously with the poet's verbal communication of it. Many passages in the poem, even when not perfectly understood, continually surprise by their delightful and beautiful inventions; I quote stanza 26 as example, in spite of its clumsy final line:

> For how to the heart's cheering
> The down-dugged ground-hugged grey
> Hovers off, the jay-blue heavens appearing
> Of pied and peeled May!
> Blue-beating and hoary-glow height; or night, still higher,
> With belled fire and the moth-soft Milky Way,
> What by your measure is the heaven of desire,
> The treasure never eyesight got, nor was ever guessed what for
> the hearing?

In spite of such directly pleasurable verse, much of the strongest part of the poem acknowledges God's power and the righteousness of his doom, in gloomy medieval tradition:

> But we dream we are rooted in earth – Dust!
> Flesh falls within sight of us, we, though our flower the same,
> Wave with the meadow, forget that there must
> The sour scythe cringe, and the blear share come.

And so, while parts of the poem predict some of the loveliest sensuous and pleasurable nature-imagery that Hopkins ever wrote – the
wonderful sonnets that he created in the countryside around St
Beuno's during the spring and summer of 1877 – the sombre tone
and voice of much of it look forward, rather, to the desolate sonnets
he composed at the end of his short life, as a lonely outsider in hostile and dreary Dublin of the late 1880s.

Seven
'Complicated but euphonious': The Welsh Language

From his second day in Wales, when in Cwm churchyard with Francis Bacon he had noticed, among names like William, Martha, Thomas, Edward, Margaret, Elizabeth, and Henry carved on tombstones, some entirely in Welsh, Hopkins had felt attracted by the language, and had wanted to learn it. When he had been in Wales less than a fortnight, from the summit of Moel-y-Parc he had looked up the Clwyd valley towards Ruthin, and had felt 'an instress and charm of Wales'. And then his journal had continued, as though it were as a consequence of that feeling about Wales: 'Indeed in coming here I began to feel a desire to do something for the conversion of Wales. I began to learn Welsh too but not with very pure intentions perhaps' (*J*, 258).

On his first confrontation with the written language he thought it consisted mostly of consonants, but after hearing it spoken he changed his mind. As he wrote to his mother: 'It is almost all vowels and they run off the tongue like oil by diphthongs and by triphthongs – there are 20 of the latter and nearly 30 of the former.' (In *Wild Wales*, George Borrow had quoted [164-5] two curious stanzas, on the coldness of the snow at the top of Snowdon, consisting entirely of vowels and the consonant *r*:

> Oer yw'r Eira ar Eryri, – o'ryw
> Ar awyr i rewi;
> Oer yw'r ia ar riw'r ri,
> A'r Eira oer yw 'Ryri.

O Ri y'Ryri yw'r oera, – o'r âr,
Ar oror wir arwa;
O'r awyr a yr Eira,
O'i ryw i roi rew a'r ia.)

He had always looked upon himself as half-Welsh, Hopkins wrote to his mother from St Beuno's, soon after his arrival. The surname Hopkins, common in south Wales, was often considered to be particularly Welsh; and Hopkins was probably assuming Welsh ancestry on no more grounds than this. Seldom over-modest, he was half-ashamed at the lack of distinction in his immediate family, and felt the need to boast of some more colourful, Celtic blood in his veins. But the name 'Hopkins' had originated in southern England (where '-kin' for some time was a popular diminutive), being recorded in Saxon Cambridgeshire before the Norman Conquest, and it had then spread into Buckinghamshire, Gloucestershire, Sussex, and Warwickshire. When in the Jesuit novitiate at Roehampton, Hopkins had noticed, carved on a marble tomb in the nearby church at Wimbledon, the Hopkins family arms, which his father had recently adopted. It was, he recalled to his mother, 'the tomb of William Mansel Phillips of Coedgair in Carmarthenshire ... and of Caroline his wife only child of Benjamin Bond Hopkins Esq' (L3, 109).

So, before he had met any Welsh people Hopkins felt himself romantically attached to them. But getting to know them was difficult. They were, he discovered,

> very civil and respectful but do not much come to us and those who are converted are for the most part not very stanch. They are much swayed by ridicule. Wesleyanism is the popular religion. They are said to have a turn for religion, especially what excites outward fervour, and more refinement and pious feeling than the English peasantry but less steadfastness and sincerity....
> I ought to say that the Welsh have the reputation also of being covetous and immoral: I add this to forestall your saying it, for, as I say, I warm to them – and in different degrees to all the Celts.
> (L3, 127)

St Beuno's stood just to the west of Offa's Dyke, whose course Hopkins must often have walked along, as it skirts several villages he visited during his three years in Wales. The Dyke had been built

111

by an old Saxon king against the incursions of the Welsh. In the 1850s George Borrow, tramping through North Wales, had met a mower who had told him that once it was customary 'for the English to cut off the ears of every Welshman who was found to the east of the dyke, and for the Welsh to hang every Englishman whom they found to the west of it' (*Borrow*, 56). The mower still believed that the English 'were ashamed to be seen walking with any people, who were not, at least, as well-dressed as themselves' (ibid, 54).

In Hopkins's time the national dress was still worn on occasion: farmers' wives might wear a scarlet cloak and beaver hat in the shape of a truncated cone when they sold butter on market days. A rector of the college a decade after Hopkins wrote that the Welsh people around them disliked foreigners, and they tried to force 'the hated Saxon or Irishman' to leave the country. 'In our vale the foreigners are never in sufficient numbers to give them any hope of making head against the Welsh, and their only safety is in meek submission' (*Hunter*, 42). St Beuno's was often called the College of Englishmen. Even the local Welsh Catholics retained their traditional anti-English feeling, which, ironically, had helped sustain Catholic opposition to the new religion in sixteenth-century Wales. Furthermore, Welsh Catholics, like Irish Catholics, had not always seen eye to eye with the Society of Jesus, whose members, unlike the secular parish priests, tended to be more loyal to their own organisation, and less inclined towards local allegiances.

The people in the district around St Beuno's normally spoke their own Celtic tongue, and English was seldom understood outside the seaside resorts, which had been developed largely by Lancashire people. Several of the first Jesuits at St Beuno's, in the early 1850s, had started learning Welsh with the intention of converting local people, and a Welsh service was instituted in the chapel, but the congregation lessened until in March 1851 it had consisted of two laundry maids and a child. After 1860 there had been few attempts at learning the language or making conversions, though there had been an occasional sensation, such as on 30 March 1854, when Miss Smalley, daughter of the Anglican parson of Cwm, had been received. A Welsh sermon was sometimes preached in the chapel, and one in 1858 had remained in people's memories, but only because it had lasted for two and a half hours ('Bygone Life and Customs at St Beuno's', *Letters and Notices* 20 [1895], 209). As to the Catholic religion, wrote Fr Hunter,

> it is commonly regarded with a feeling of intense but unreasoning hatred. 'I do not know why it is, but we hate you worse than we hate the devil' was the candid avowal once made by a Welshman to a Catholic ... [though] I never heard of a Catholic suffering for his religion at the hands of people of the lower class. Among the respectable members of society, examples of downright bigotry are not unknown.
> (*Hunter*, 43)

Although conversions to the faith were rare, it was known that sham conversions of the Welsh to the faith could readily be secured for a small amount of money. 'When really converted', said Fr Hunter, 'they seem to make excellent Catholics.'

By the 1870s a wish such as Hopkins's to convert the Welsh had come to be regarded as naive by older members of the community. Now and then practical schemes had been suggested, such as that 'pamphlets be distributed over the countryside, telling the Welsh people about old Catholic Wales, its customs and ceremonies, martyrs, hymns, churches, and shrines.' Only the year before Hopkins arrived there it had been reported that at St Beuno's on 12 May 1873,

> Father Macdonnell has commenced to-day what we hope will be a Welsh Seminary, for boys speaking Welsh and showing a disposition for the priesthood. The first pupil is from St Asaph, he is at present to come to the College every day at 7 o'clock, to dine, &c., here and return home at night.

But these schemes, like all the others, had quickly fallen through.

The St Beuno's training was of a practical nature and, on consulting his Rector on the first day of his annual retreat, Hopkins was discouraged from learning the Welsh language 'unless it were purely for the sake of labouring among the Welsh'. Reluctantly he gave it up, though, as he confided to his journal, 'I had no sooner given up the Welsh than my desire seemed to be for the conversion of Wales and I had it in mind to give up everything else for that' (*J*, 258).

However, in spite of his Rector's disapproval and his own scruples and decision to give up the language, only five months later his journal revealed that he was taking Welsh lessons from a Miss Susannah Jones, a Catholic of local farming stock who lived near the Rhuallt crossroads. Somehow or other Hopkins had again taken up learning the Welsh language, in spite of the sanctions and contrary decisions. He must have convinced himself that, after all, his learning of the language could be justified, and had then sought and obtained permission from his Rector; there is no precise evidence as to the process the change of his own or his Rector's mind took. The St Beuno's records and his own journal and letters do not mention any Welsh sermon of his, or even his visiting the Welsh-speaking people, but the importance he placed upon his learning the language even while his official studies harassed him can be seen from a letter he wrote to Bridges in February 1875: '[My studies leave] me time for hardly anything: the course is very hard, it must be said. Nevertheless I have tried to learn a little Welsh, in reality one of the hardest of languages' (L1, 31).

The impression is that his enthusiasm for Welsh had allied itself with his strong wilfulness to pressurise people and events into producing the required resumption of the language, whatever form the surface arguments took. Hopkins's intense scrupulosity towards his own personal behaviour sometimes cohabited with a convenient naive unawareness of his deeper motivations. In the same letter he also mentions that, despite all the various scholarly reading his official studies gave him no time for, 'I can, at all events a little, read Duns Scotus' (L1, 31). As he must have known well, from the Catholic history of fights between the prescribed Thomism and the breakaway Scotism, Scotus would not have been considered relevant to his course.

Whatever were his stated reasons for learning Welsh, it soon emerged that he associated the language with poetry and with legend, considering it some sort of formally realised amalgam of poetic abstractions. His journal for 7 February 1875 shows him enthusiastically exploring this new world deep in fairies and queer etymology. It must have been a strange scene in the cottage near the Rhuallt crossroads, three-quarters of a mile from the college: a Welsh

Catholic 'good woman' (as Hopkins called her), Miss Jones, encouraging the short and nervous Fr Hopkins to convert *Cinderella* into Welsh, and in return the Oxford-English priest encouraging the lady teacher to deviate from vocabulary and grammar into more seductive subjects. He asked her the Welsh for fairy, and

> She told me *cipenaper* (or perhaps *cipernaper*, *Anglice kippernapper*): the word is nothing but *kidnapper*.... However in coming to an understanding between ourselves what fairies (she says *fairess* by the way for a she-fairy) and kippernappers were, on my describing them as little people 'that high', she told me quite simply that she had seen them.

At haymaking time, early one morning she had been climbing the slope of the Rhuallt road to get to her grandfather's farm, when 'she saw three little boys of about four years old wearing little frock coats and odd little caps running and dancing before her, taking hands and going round, then going further, still dancing and always coming together, she said.' She took no notice of them, but when she reached the house she told them what she had seen, and 'wondered that children could be out so early. "Why she has seen the kippernappers" her grandmother said to her son, Susannah Jones' father' (*J*, 263).

Sadly, Hopkins's extant journals finish at that point; but his description of the lesson shows that his imagination, as well as that of Miss Jones, had been enlivened well beyond the usual expectations of a language class. Even the vocabulary footnotes he put to this account add to its colour, rather than taking the reader back to the dictionary: 'She afterwards called the coats long (*llaes*, that is / trailing; perhaps unconfined by a girdle) and black. The caps or hats were round and black.'

He was not only learning to speak and write Welsh, but was also practising writing poetry in the language. A translation into Welsh of St Francis Xavier's Hymn, 'O Deus, ego amo te', found among his possessions after his death and probably written by him, shows the naked encounter between his hungry Muse and the strict regulations of a foreign language still only partly absorbed. The metre is not Welsh but English. There are linguistic mistakes, such as a reflexive verb misused, an irregular verb conjugated wrongly, a lack of familiarity with everyday idioms. But with 'The Wreck of the Deutschland' in mind there are two specific deviations from normal Welsh usage which show how Hopkins, though ignorant, could force the Welsh to accommodate his strong artistic needs. In lines one and two of the third stanza he uses a device *sangiad*, disruption of the conventional prose word order, to change 'Aneirif ddolur a phoen chwŷs darfu it eu dwyn' to 'Aneirif ddolur darfu it',/ A phoen, a chwŷs eu dwyn' ('Endless grief hast thou, and pain and sweat, endured'). In other words he wanted *darfu* next to *ddolur*, and also a structure of parallels with 'A phoen, a chwŷs'. This is contrary to correct Welsh practice, which requires that the two parts of the compound verb *darfu* and *dwyn* should be near each other. Similarly, Hopkins omitted a desirable conjunctive pronoun from stanza five, and disrupted normal Welsh sentence-structure, by placing next to each other *garaf* and *garu'r*, the two parts of the verb 'to love', so that their simultaneous difference and similarity can be emphasized (Dr T. Parry in *The Poems of Gerard Manley Hopkins*, fourth edition, edited by W.H. Gardner and N.H. MacKenzie [London, 1967], 324-25.)

Hopkins's comparative ignorance of the language helped him to use Welsh in part to form abstract sound- and rhythm-patterns to suit his own poetic purposes. The loneliness of his Welsh studies may have helped, in that he probably had no language authority, apart from a couple of outdated books and Miss Jones (who in all likelihood was not familiar with poetic practices) to stop his pattern-forming with the true but destructive judgement that his language was 'wrong'. If correct grammar and the desires of his poetic muse were opposed, his circumstances were allowing the latter to win. His nonconformity nearly always benefited his poetry, even when, as it did increasingly deeply, it caused him personal hurt. It was not any communicative properties of the Welsh language that he wanted but its licence to use new poetic enrichments, whether they existed in the real language or only in his imaginative version of it.

In the most balanced account we have of Hopkins's poetic indebtedness to Welsh (see Bibliography), Gweneth Lilly writes that even if Hopkins had never studied Welsh poetry, 'his mature work would have contained instances of internal rhyme, half-rhyme, and alliteration', and that one of the main Welsh features that influenced Hopkins, *cynghanedd*, 'appears to have accorded with some inherent quality in his own mind'. Certainly characteristics which Hopkins found in Welsh poetry developed emphases already evident in the lecture-notes he had made during his teaching year at Roehampton. For the lessons he had given to the Jesuit juniors Hopkins had collected together and written down his accumulated ideas on the major characteristics of verse, probably based on a paper 'The Science of Poetry' he had read to the Hexameron Essay Society at Oxford University ten years before, and which had been wasted until now.

The opening emphasis of his lecture on 'Poetry and Verse' had been that poetry was a special form of spoken *sound*; a printed or written version of a poem was only its representation, not its actuality: 'Poetry is speech framed for contemplation of the mind by way of hearing.' 'Matter and meaning' were only subordinate features of poetry, of secondary importance to its frame and shape. The shape of poetry 'is contemplated for its own sake'. Poetry was in fact 'speech only employed to carry the inscape of speech for the inscape's sake'. The inscape of the poem's words had to be emphasized in preference to their matter and meaning; 'the inscape must be dwelt on'. In order to make the inscape understood, 'repetition, *oftening, over-and-overing, aftering* of the inscape must take place in order to detach it to the mind' from the less important sounds which surrounded it in the poem. Poetry, therefore, as Hopkins saw it, had to be 'speech which afters and oftens its inscape, speech couched in a repeating figure' (*J*, 289). The dominant importance given in Hopkins's mature poetry to repetition itself went back to Hopkins's earliest days at Oxford, when he had made lists of words with similar sounds and meanings.

This emphatic view of the nature of poetry is the language of a poet rather than a pedant; Hopkins was thinking of what his own poetry would be were he to write any. In another lecture from the same time, 'Rhythm and other Structural Parts' (*J*, 267-88), Hopkins isolated a group of 'repeating figures' which he called 'lettering of syllables': 'Likeness or sameness of letters [,] and this some or all [,] and these vowels or consonants [,] and initial or final'. 'Rhyme' had, he said, a 'more special or narrower sense', and so he used to describe this likeness the terms 'widely rhyme' or 'chime'. Assonance, alliteration, and 'skothending' (final half-rhyme), were all forms of this 'rhyme in a wide sense'. He gave as example a translation of four lines of Norse poetry which is very similar to both Welsh poetry and to his own later practice:

> Softly now are sifting
> Snows on landscape frozen.
> Thickly fall the flakelets,
> Feathery-light together.

(Compare 'The Wreck of the Deutschland', 4: 'I am soft sift'.) At Roehampton Hopkins had, as Lilly says, 'already a keen interest in poetic devices resembling those which he later found in Welsh verse'.

Welsh lessons probably lasted, on and off, until about September 1876, when Grace Hopkins agreed to obtain for her brother a 'nice glazed table-portrait of the Pope' (L3, 141), as a farewell gift for Miss Jones. There then appears to be a gap until the following April, when Hopkins mentions going to stay with Miss Jones's brother at Caernarvon, to better his Welsh. His active involvement with the language, then, lasted nearly three years, from his first week at St Beuno's at least until four months before he left.

As well as writing occasional religious poetry and learning spoken Welsh, Hopkins was also searching out examples of classical Welsh poetry. In July 1875 he noticed printed in Welsh in a local newspaper, *The Montgomery Mercury*, the sixteenth-century bard Tudur Aled's 'Cywydd to St Winefride' (*Cywydd i Wenfrewi Santes*), with a translation and commentary. When he came to write his English verse-play 'St Winefred's Well' he took some of the Welsh language echoes from this Cywydd. Moreover in his own Cywydd on his bishop's Silver Jubilee, where he uses the legend of Winefride and Beuno, there are several similarities with Tudur Aled's poem. (Hopkins was writing this 'Cywydd' at the same time as 'The Wreck of the Deutschland', in Spring 1876, and probably finished it before the English poem was complete.)

David Jones (*Letters to a Friend*, ed. Aneirin Talfan Davies

[Swansea, 1980]) is mistaken in considering that Hopkins was attracted by the 'exacting nature' of Welsh metrical forms which '"chimed" in his mind with the exacting discipline which ... was a pronounced element in his own psychology'. On the contrary Hopkins's 'Cywydd' is accurate only in the fairly simple metre. In his attempt at including *cynghanedd*, the complex regulations governing internal rhyme and alliteration, he is correct in only two of the eighteen lines. Again, Hopkins was not lastingly attracted by the rhythm of the *cywydd* form, which was, in fact, cramped by the same number of *syllables* – seven – in every single line. In 'The Wreck of the Deutschland' Hopkins's new rhythm worked by disciplining the *stresses* in a line, but allowing extraordinary freedom in the number of syllables, however many were convenient. What attracted Hopkins was the *cynghanedd*'s various systems of enriching and binding verse, so that against a poem's background of haphazard sounds governed by words chosen primarily for their rightness of meaning, an inscape of decorative sound-patterns is foregrounded. Hopkins later admitted there was a danger that the sense would suffer; but, he insisted, his poetry had to be read aloud, so that the full effect of the inscape of sound-patterning was the primary concern of the audience ('those who hear').

In some ways Hopkins's practice was a reversion to an older, more richly systematic and rhetorical kind of alliterative verse, such as Old English verse had been. But *cynghanedd*'s alliterative rules were stricter; for instance a practice Hopkins often followed was in alliterating the two halves of a line or a shorter unit, so that several consonants were repeated in the same order in the second half as had occurred in the first ('of the Yore-flood, of the year's fall'). Hopkins did not, however, want to lose out on meaning, and his best mature poetry, from 'The Wreck of the Deutschland' onwards, has as primary characteristic the typical Hopkinsian 'astringent, tense relation between sound and meaning'. In the 'Wreck' one does not find patterns of pre-ordained sound interrupting the flow of meaning; on the contrary, the poem largely works by making a series of outrageous challenges on the listener to find such conflicts, and forcing his acknowledgement of the poet's incredible technical success in avoiding them.

It would be wrong to say that Hopkins *copied* Welsh conventions in 'The Wreck of the Deutschland'. Copying would have deadened his verse, but Welsh enlivened it with fresh fuel. There were several reasons. A greater variety of effect was possible in the more developed and complex English language. Hopkins's stress-timed 'sprung rhythm' was a remarkable freedom almost opposite in effect to the finically puritanical restrictions of syllabic Welsh verse; and mainly, Hopkins used what he wanted of *cynghanedd* when he wanted it and adapted to his own purposes, rather than being governed by all its complex rules. The following examples (adapting Lilly's and Gardner's [see Bibliography] definitions and examples) of Hopkins's most common usages of *cynghanedd* also show his powers of imaginative variation and wilful liberation from *cynghanedd*:

a) *Cynghanedd draws* ('the first part of the line alliterates with the last part, there being a portion in the middle which is ... passed over'):

Tudur Aled, *Cywydd i Wenfrewi*, line 10:

   'Min i gledd dryw i mwnwgl ai'
   1 2 3   1 2 3

Hopkins, 'Cywydd', line 1 (but note the many additional chiming patterns):

   'Y mae'n llewyn yma'n llon'
   1 23   4 1 2 3 4

Hopkins, 'The Wreck of the Deutschland', st. 23:

   'To bathe in his fall-gold mercies, to breathe in his all-fire glances.'
   1 2 3 4 5 6 7 8 9 10   11 12 1 2   3 4 5 6 7 8 9 10 11 12

Gardner gives this as 'a close approximation' to *cynghanedd draws*, using the whole word 'mercies' as the passed-over middle, and finds only six alliterations in each half-line; the full count of twelve shows how remarkably elaborate Hopkins could make a pattern without losing out on sense – the effect is all the more powerful because of the scale of the technical challenge.

b) *Cynghanedd* effect: 'The Wreck of the Deutschland', st. 25 (but using several kinds of English word-play in addition):

'Is it love in her of the being as her lover had been?'

'The Wreck of the Deutschland', st. 2:

'The swoon of a heart that the sweep and the hurl of thee trod'
  1   2   3   4 5 1 2   3   4   5

c) *Cynghanedd sain* ('the line is divided into three parts; the end of the first part rhymes with the end of the second part, while the second and third parts are bound together by alliteration'):

Hopkins, 'Cywydd': 'Gwan ddwfr a ddwg, nis dwg dŷn'

'The Wreck of the Deutschland', st. 26 (further enriched by other *cynghanedd* and additional alliteration):

'The down-dugged ground-hugged grey'
    1   2   1   2

'The Wreck of the Deutschland', st. 21 (alliteration in third and first parts, rather than third and second):

'Banned by the land of their birth'.

'The Wreck of the Deutschland', st. 34 (Gardner gives one three-fold alliteration, missing the full thunderous complexity of the two-fold *thr* alliteration and the four-fold *th*):

'He in three of the thunder-throne!'

This device, with many variations, is very common in Hopkins's mature poetry, from the 1877 sonnets to the Dublin poems. It even comes in the 'dark' sonnets ('that toil, that coil, since (seems) I kissed', in the poem 'Not, I'll not, carrion comfort'); and also occurs in Hopkins's last poem: 'bears, cares and combs'. Among other devices which Lilly notices as probably adapted from the Welsh are: internal rhyme combined with alliteration; the penultimate syllable of a line rhyming with a preceding word, with the last two syllables accented ('call of the tall nun'); and alliteration of pairs of initial consonants and of medial consonants ('cipher of suffering Christ'). Hopkins's later, desperate, division of a compound word ('Wind-lilylocks-laced', in 'Harry Ploughman'), and 'running-over' rhymes ('leeward/ . . . drew her/ Dead', in 'The Wreck of the Deutschland', 14) were also sanctioned in Welsh practice.

Gardner goes too far in finding a technical Welsh name for every little poetic heightening of Hopkins's, who (lacking a teacher or textbooks) probably spent less time than Gardner would have us believe in close study and note-taking of *cynghanedd* rules and varieties, and more in getting hold of the rough rules of two or three devices, a few general principles, and, in the main, thinking of the possibilities created by them for his own, essentially English, works. Hopkins did not copy influences (with the odd exception of Swinburne in 'Ad Mariam', see *W*, 202) but, as he later insisted, admired them 'and did otherwise'. Finding other similarities between Welsh and Hopkins's poetry, Gardner assumes Welsh to be the source, when it may not be. He quotes, for instance, a linguist who says that in Welsh: 'such minor but useful parts of speech as articles, prepositions, pronouns and the copula are freely dispensed with'. It seems obvious that the classicist Hopkins would not have needed to look further than the Latin he already had to have realised that languages could work with fewer words than English took. Similarly the comparative syntactical freedom of Welsh was shared, because it naturally happens in inflected languages generally, with Latin, which Hopkins knew before – and a great deal better than – Welsh. Then the most obvious source of compound words is German, not Welsh.

In general, however, Hopkins was helped by the various chiming devices of Welsh poetics to escape from unforceful poetry, and from purely ornamental devices. As Gweneth Lilly says, Hopkins 'recognised in the devices of *cynghanedd* a means of making the language of poetry more forcible, of giving to the common speech on which it is founded the heightened emphasis of rhetoric.' Welsh devices were not ornamental, but joined 'with the rhythm to give additional weight and prominence to significant words', thus providing a means of fetching out the required inscapes. Unlike Gardner, Lilly estimates the limitations of the Welsh influence on Hopkins, remarking that many of his poetic effects though derived from *cynghanedd* would not be possible in Welsh verse, 'where the poet is obliged to maintain a more or less uniform level of intricacy throughout a poem.' Hopkins, on the other hand, Lilly continues acutely, alternates 'with a plainer style, which offsets its elaboration and forms an astonishing and brilliant variety of texture.' Hopkins experimented with and adapted his materials 'to suit his own purposes, transmuting them until we almost lose sight of the original elements.'

Eight
The Crow of Maenefa

In late Spring of the next year, 1876, Hopkins completed 'The Wreck of the Deutschland', and wrote to Fr Henry Coleridge, whom he considered his 'oldest friend in the Society', telling him of the poem. Coleridge had been editor of the Jesuit periodical *The Month* for more than ten years, and during that time had been the first to publish Newman's *The Dream of Gerontius*. Before he had read the poem, Coleridge was asked by Hopkins to accept it for publication. 'I had to tell him that I felt sure he wd. personally dislike it very much, only that he was to consider not his tastes but those of the *Month's* readers'. Coleridge replied that if it 'rhymed and scanned and construed and did not make nonsense or bad morality', he did not see why it should not appear in the July 1876 number of *The Month* (*L3*, 138).

So Coleridge received a copy, heavily marked with accents, to guide its reading. But he 'read the poem and could not understand it, and he did not relish publishing any poem that he himself could not master'. He prevaricated, first saying it would appear in the August issue, as long as Hopkins agreed to cut the accents, and then sent no further progress reports, so that by mid-September Hopkins was forced to acknowledge rejection. 'They dared not print it', he said (*L2*, 15). Apart from the hurt he must have felt at the literary incomprehension and evasive personal behaviour of an old friend, Hopkins saw the rejection as of more than the poem itself or its literary methods. And from this point on he often had a sense of having enemies in the higher ranks of the Society, and official disapproval, which were reinforced when he failed his theology exam

124

at the end of his stay in Wales, thereby being downgraded in his future professional career.

Hopkins did not wish 'The Wreck of the Deutschland' to appear under his own name, and when he submitted it for publication chose to call himself 'Brân Maenefa', the Crow of Maenefa, a Welsh bardic pseudonym which he also used for the 'Cywydd' he composed for the elaborately decorated album presented to Bishop James Brown on his Silver Jubilee visit to St Beuno's in July 1876. Why did Hopkins choose this name for himself?

To allow a poem to make its own way, but with the name of its author hidden under a pseudonym, fits in both with a common habit of professional-class nineteenth-century authors, especially clerical ones, who wished to maintain an undemonstrative exterior image, and also with Hopkins's own scruples about the delicate place of art in his profession. But why 'The Crow of Maenefa'?

To trace the origins of this personal mask we have to go back to the Hopkins family, to Gerard's father Manley, who in his youth was friendly with Thomas Hood the Elder, poet, humourist, and author of one of the most well-known Victorian ballads, 'The Song of the Shirt'. Manley Hopkins had introduced his children to Hood's poems, and they grew up with Hood's sense of humour as some standard for their own jokes and word-juggling (*W*, 12-13, 19).

One form of verbal joke which Gerard Hopkins developed with increasing elaborateness throughout his adult life, that of calling himself a crow or rook, seems to have originated in a family habit of referring to each other as a type of bird. Madeline House described how, after the death in 1952 of Lionel, the last survivor of the Hopkins family, she and her husband Humphry looked through The Garth, Haslemere, the family home, just before its contents were finally dispersed. Among a large trove of invaluable Hopkins family material was found 'a *jeu d'esprit* called "The Prize Prophecy Album, sole contributors the Falcon and the Swallow", evidently Arthur and Everard [two of Gerard's brothers] – an elaborately worked out game about racing' (*HRB* 5 [1974], 34-5, and *HRB* 6 [1975], 17-21).

As a boy at Highgate School Hopkins was particularly influenced by Marcus Clarke, his companion in jokes and literary and

artistic ventures, who had a gift for telling grotesque stories, sometimes in verse. Among Clarke's extant early verse is a tale for which
Hopkins drew a frontispiece illustration, 'The Lady of Lynn' or 'The
Eve of St John', in which the heroine, 'that woman of sin', sees
advancing up the church aisle her future husband, tall, 'grewsome'
and 'grim', with a neck 'like some foul vulture's, so long and thin'.
He mounts the pulpit. Then,

> With two long green hands, he smoothed his bands
> And puffed out his big black gown
> As he mouthed out the text from a big black book
> He looked like some big, black, eldritch rook.
>   (W, 30-1)

Shipped off to Australia at the age of seventeen, Clarke there
became a prolific writer, constantly mentioning Hopkins in his stories. His most well-known novel, *His Natural Life*, starts in the parts
of Hampstead in which he and Hopkins had strolled together. The
hero Rufus Dawes meets at sea 'the Crow', an unlikely convict who
is a thinly disguised Hopkins: 'the slimly-made, effeminate Crow',
who 'made up for his flaccid muscles and nerveless frame by a cat-
like cunning and a spirit of devilish volatility that nothing could
subdue'. Later the Crow rubbed 'his thin hands with eldritch
[weird, frightful] glee' (*His Natural Life* [originally published 1870-
72, this version Oxford, 1997], 62, 78.)

The idea of a black-gowned cleric resembling a crow or rook took
on significance later in Hopkins's life, when he was a Jesuit. It was
a common anti-clerical image in nineteenth-century English culture.
For instance, in the opening chapters of *The Mystery of Edwin Drood*,
Dickens's last novel, published in 1870, rooks above the cathedral at
Cloisterham are compared with 'diverse venerable persons of rook-
like aspect dispersing' after a service (ch. 2), and with 'hoarser and
less distinct [human clerical] rooks in the stalls far beneath' (ch. 3).
It would not be surprising also if the vulture cleric in 'The Lady of
Lynn' alluded to John 'Vulture' Hopkins, an ancestor who had been
mentioned in Pope's *Moral Essay* 'Of the Use of Riches', and who
was known to the keenly genealogist Hopkins family. In a letter to
his mother of 30 December 1869 Hopkins reported seeing 'Vulture'

Hopkins's tombstone in Wimbledon churchyard, and remarked: 'One wd. not wish to have anything to do with the bird' (L3, 109).

In March 1860, possibly about the same time as Clarke was writing 'The Lady of Lynn', Hopkins was awarded the annual poetry prize at Highgate School for 'The Escorial', and beneath the title of that poem he wrote the self-deprecating motto from Theocritus, 'βατραχος δὲ ποτ' ακρίδας ὥς τις ἐρίσδω': compared with that of better poets, his voice is like that of a frog trying to rival the cicadas. This is the first usage in his extant writings of a fauna image when comparing himself to those about him. But in June 1865, just before his twenty-first birthday, at a time when he was tortured with self-doubt, Hopkins compared in a poem his own 'unholy' qualities with 'the sweet living' of his friends, and used the image 'Eye-greeting doves bright-counter to the rook' ('Myself unholy', 1-3). It is possible that he borrowed this from Thomas Hood's poem 'The Doves and the Crows', but the dove/crow (or raven) comparison as polar opposites had long been common in literature. In Shakespeare, for example: 'Who will not change a raven for a dove?' (MND, II.ii.113); 'I'll sacrifice the lamb that I do love,/ To spite a raven's heart within a dove' (Twelfth Night, V.i.128-9); 'So shows a snowy dove trooping with crows' (R&J, I.v.48); also 'And I will make thee think thy swan a crow' (R&J, I.ii.89).

Compared with animals, which he scarcely seemed to notice, Hopkins was peculiarly aware of birds (see pp. 61-64), and they frequently appear in his early journals, though, as with plants and trees, he never developed the common Victorian ability to name them swiftly and accurately. During the Easter vacation from Oxford, in March 1864, for instance, he

> walked to Edgware from Hampstead and home by Hendon, stopping at Kingsbury Water a quarter of an hour or so. Saw what was probably a heron: it settled on a distant elm, was driven away by two rooks, settled on a still more distant, the same thing happened, the rooks pursuing it.
>
> (J, 20)

Here Hopkins demonstrates his conformity with the common prejudice that the crow family is characterised by malevolence, destructiveness, and a generally low and common nature, particularly when compared with something nobler and rarer, like a heron. The same denigration of the crow's character arises in lines seventeen to eighteen of a poem written in Oxford in 1879, 'The Bugler's First Communion', where a guardian angel is asked by the poet to scatter the hellish forces of evil besetting the virginal bugler: 'Frowning and forefending angel-warder/ Squander the hell-rook ranks sally to molest him'.

The constant use of birds in his poems dates from Hopkins's time training at St Beuno's. Within eleven of the thirteen poems written in 1877, the *annus mirabilis* of his Welsh poetry, he focuses on birds: birds' wings in 'God's Grandeur', 'In the Valley of the Elwy', 'Pied Beauty', and 'Hurrahing in Harvest', flake-doves in 'The Starlight Night', kingfishers ('As kingfishers catch fire'), thrush ('Spring'), skylark in 'The Sea and the Skylark' and 'The Caged Skylark', kestrel ('The Windhover'), and doves in 'Ad Reverendum Patrem Fratrem Thomam Burke O.P. Collegium S. Beunonis Invisentem'. This Latin poem commemorates the visit to St Beuno's of the famous Dominican preacher Fr Thomas Burke, itinerant in the Order of Preachers' tradition. This was no ordinary presentation piece. It started with a private joke: 'in the whiteness of his clothing he was nearer than we are to the guileless doves' – 'we' being, Hopkins implies, black-clothed crows. When Hopkins wrote poetry in towns and about his inner world the birds disappeared.

The day that Hopkins first arrived at St Beuno's he had learned a good deal about the lore of the college. In its forty-year history its higgledy-piggledy buildings and extensive gardens, perched halfway up and dominated by the bare mountain Maenefa, had developed expressive names suitable to their peculiarities. Unique to St Beuno's were the Crows' Nests, seats up the tall trees in front of the college; they were probably something to do with Hopkins's friend, the colourful, bearded Schomberg Kerr, called in the Jesuits by his other, more saint-like name, Henry. Even as a Jesuit Henry Kerr commonly used naval terms when speaking, and because of his unique supervisory experience was often put in charge of teams of men. On a ship the Crow's Nest was the term used for the box fitted to the mast-head, which served as a perch and shelter for the look-out man. (Another part of the St Beuno's gardens, known as the Quarter-Deck, probably also owed its name to Henry Kerr.) It seems unlikely that Hopkins would not have climbed into the Crows' Nests, as since his childhood he had been known as a climber: of the trees in his Oak Hill garden, and as a Jesuit at Stonyhurst College of goalposts and a perilous ledge on the wall of a residential block.

The day after he arrived at St Beuno's, in the brief account of the college he had written to his father, Hopkins had included information about the Crows' Nests (*L3*, 124). Two days later, in a letter to his mother, he had related how he and Henry Kerr had met the eighty-eight-year-old lodge-keeper of Brynbella, Mrs Piozzi's home, who had told him that 'she was a Tremeirchion Cow ... all the places about have their own beast; there are the Cwm Calves, the Denbigh Cats, the Caerwys Crows' (*L3*, 125). The traditional learned explanation for characterising a parish's inhabitants by animal nicknames is given in the *History of the Diocese of St Asaph*, published in the same year, 1874, which cites Brain, Cathod, Cacwn, Cwn, Malwod, and Ŵyn (crows [or rooks or ravens], cats, wasps or wild bees, dogs, snails, and lambs) as 'in reality the emblems, and it may be the pagan totems, of the chiefs and their tribes' (*DRT*, i.2). Less learning and more commonsense, however, suggests otherwise. Such nick-naming is still, in the 1990s, current in this area of North Wales – Ruthin Dogs, for instance – and obviously relates to local rivalries and prejudices. A lady of a family which has lived in the St Beuno's district for several hundred years commented to me in 1996 that the lodgekeeper was 'probably a very shrewd woman'. 'Caerwys people have always been judgmental', her understanding of 'Crows'. 'Denbigh Cats' she finds straightforwardly descriptive of a kind of person, and calves are gentle but rather stupid. In Hopkins's time, she said, 'the people around here used to be markedly inbred, so that tribal features were noticeable'. Such features could be physical (I heard it said in 1996 by a valley dweller in this area that mountain people are recognisable by their long arms and short legs), or moral/mental (memories of medieval teaching, exemplified in bestiaries, where types of birds and animals were said to possess human qualities, and therefore to provide lessons for humans).

Hopkins wondered about a similar name for himself, and chose the 'Crow of Maenefa', or, in Welsh, Brân Maenefa. There were two possible sources for this name. From 1870 to 1873 he had studied philosophy at St Mary's Hall, Stonyhurst, in Lancashire. Although his time there in the main had not been spent at the neighbouring Stonyhurst College, a secondary school for boys aged ten to eighteen, but in the separate Juniorate community hidden away in the woods, he would nevertheless have come into contact with the college pupils, probably substituting for the masters on occasion. Among the schoolboys a common nickname for their Jesuit masters was 'crows', referring to their black garb and flapping sleeves. (Hopkins no doubt recalled Clarke's poem 'The Lady of Lynn'.) A second reason for choosing 'the Crow of Maenefa' would be that in the St Beuno's grounds the two most raucous bird-sounds to be heard were (and still are) those of the rooks and the hawks, although there were several other kinds of birds about. And the mountain of Maenefa seems, in fact, to be inhabited only by these two kinds of bird, the hawks nesting on the ground and the rooks in the tops of the clumps of pines.

When Hopkins came to write poetry at St Beuno's, heavily influenced by his reading of verse in the Welsh bardic tradition, and also hesitant about the egoism it would show if he assigned his own name to his poetry ('you must never say the poem is mine', he told his mother) (L3, 139), he chose as his personal yet disguised bardic signature 'Brân Maenefa'. This signature accompanies the 'Cywydd' written in April 1876, and also 'The Wreck of the Deutschland', written during the spring of the same year. In the Oxford English Texts *Hopkins* Norman MacKenzie mentions Dr T. Parry's note in the third edition of Hopkins's poems (327, 353-4) that 'Brân' is 'probably taken from the character in the second branch of The Mabinogi, *Bendigaid Fran*, Brân the Blessed'. MacKenzie comments that Hopkins could only have meant this ironically, as Brân in the *Mabinogion* was a colossal giant while Hopkins was very short. I think that while Hopkins may easily have come across the name Brân in his foragings among Welsh literature, and indeed may have consciously used this association as a secondary (and humorous) obfuscating device, his primary and more personal reason was that the straightforward meaning of 'brân' is *crow* or *rook*. As opposed to the kestrel, or windhover, which in its glory is the 'king-/ dom of daylight's dauphin', Hopkins resembles the *other*, lower (i.e., morally, aesthetically, and physically – down the hill), Maenefa bird, the crow, both in his coarse common attempts at language and in his laughable, flapping black-stuff clothing. Hopkins may be recalling traditions of lessons humans can draw from the animal world: in a medieval bestiary, in the Bodleian library, the hawk is 'the image of the holy man who seizes the Kingdom of God' (cf. 'I caught ... king-/ dom of daylight's dauphin'), while the raven 'signifies the blackness of sinners'. If Tremeirchion (the nearest village to St Beuno's) had its Cows, and Cwm (a few miles away) its Calves, Maenefa had, much more fittingly, its actual bird and human inhabitants, its Crows, of which Hopkins was one.

When Hopkins was moved to Stonyhurst College in 1882 to teach classics at the school, although he wrote there the serious poems 'Ribblesdale' and 'The Leaden Echo and the Golden Echo', ironically the only poems which he published while at the college were three triolets in the school magazine, 'The Child is Father to the Man', 'No news in the *Times* today', and 'Cockle's Antibilious Pills', poems which he admitted 'have the taint of jest' (*L1*, 178). As was the custom for members of staff whose work appeared in *The Stonyhurst Magazine*, they were printed under a pseudonym, and Hopkins chose 'Bran'. At Stonyhurst he was still a Crow, a gowned Jesuit teacher, but no longer a Maenefan one.

In the light of his already complex use of the crow image, an undercurrent of personal humour may be detected in his remark in a letter to his mother of March 1876 which describes how he and another Jesuit, Richard Clarke, 'made one of the only two couples that reached Moel Fammau' (*L3*, 137), in the Clwydian range of mountains. He modestly wrote that the mountain was 'distant as the crow flies about nine miles'. As the crow flies it is actually seven and a half miles, but as the two Crows walked it was at least twenty miles, in bad weather, and including the climb of a snow-covered mountain.

The one person that we know for certain was familiar with the name's significance for Hopkins was his friend Robert Bridges.

Bridges was sent copies of all the poems signed 'Bran' and 'Brân Maenefa', and besides, Hopkins makes three mentions of crows in his extant letters to Bridges which appear to refer humorously to the same nom-de-plume. Firstly, when Hopkins had been at St Beuno's for six months, he wrote to Bridges: 'a long crow-flight is between us [i.e., distance in a straight line, and distance I, the crow, would have to travel] – one over which the crow-quill ['A steel pen for fine writing' (OED)], to follow the lead of my own thoughts, does not carry' (L1, 30). Bridges had assumed that Hopkins was still stationed at Roehampton, a mere tram-ride from his own London house, and had sent an invitation to Hopkins to dine with him. But when the letter caught up with him, the crow had flown, Hopkins having moved from Roehampton to Wales – 'a long crow-flight' indeed. And then a letter of 25 May 1888 which shows that the joke must have been kept up between them over a long period starts: 'Bridges, have at you. Not a low, not a crow, not a bark, not a bray from either of us has crossed the [St George's] Channel this long while. I am presently going gently to crow [i.e., brag], but first....' Then towards the end of the same letter he writes: 'But I have had one hit. Of this I meekly bray and mildly crow' (L1, 274, 277).

*   *   *

The crow image is also prominent in Schubert's song-cycle *Die Winterreise*, 'The Winter Journey'. In 'Frühlingstraum' ('Dream of Spring'), the Wanderer is rudely awakened from his blissful lilting dream of gay blossoms and green meadows in May by the discordant crowing of cocks – 'my eyes opened, it was cold and dark, and the crows croaked on the roof'. The cock's noise is 'krähten', from 'Krähe', a crow, and is symbolic of malevolence and a warning. After a respite, the crow image appears again, in the second part of the cycle, in a mournful, C minor, song, 'Die Krähe', where, as Gerald Moore says, 'the treble in the accompaniment throughout this sinister song is like the flapping wings of the bird': 'A crow has been following me since I left the town, flying above my head. Crow, strange creature that you are, will you not leave me alone?' Crazed, the wanderer decides to accept as companion the crow he cannot avoid, until his bones are ready to be picked clean by the bird. 'Die

Krähe' is followed by a heart-rending song 'Letzte Hoffnung' ('Last Hope').

The crow in these two songs plays a traditional mystical role which goes back well before the nineteenth century; there are traditional English and French songs, such as 'The Carnal [=crow, from French *corneille*] and the Crane', in which birds tell of the birth of Christ.

So when Hopkins called himself the Crow of Maenefa he was also referring to an image of wandering and mystical sign-telling. From his earliest times in the Jesuits, but particularly during his three years at St Beuno's, there is the constant sense, as there is in Schubert's 'Frühlingstraum', of the homeless outcast, constantly wandering, and dreaming, involuntarily, of nature and the countryside, and being cruelly woken up to be reminded of his real life and responsibilities, the harsh reality of the daily, tiring and health-destroying, work he had – his official studies and duties.

Nine
'Wild Wales breathes poetry'

In 'The Wreck of the Deutschland' Hopkins wrote as he had never written before; he also wrote as he would never write again. No poem of his after this was anything like as long, ambitious, experimental, or time-consuming; he felt his poetry to be under a cloud. Its rejection for publication, and the official disapproval which could be inferred from that rejection, shows how unsuited was the Society of Jesus at that time to original poetry and to the genius of Gerard Hopkins. (A Franciscan has suggested to me that his order would have been more suitable for Hopkins and sympathetic to his poetry.)

At the same time as he was composing 'The Wreck of the Deutschland', Hopkins was working, with some hesitations and difficulties, on the very different task of poems in three languages, English, Latin, and Welsh, to celebrate the silver jubilee of the local bishop. And of the three the one which best deserves mention, in spite of its inaccurate Welsh, is the 'Cywydd', which (even in translation) conveys some of Hopkins's deep feelings for Wales:

> Our focal point here is bright and glad with the streamlet of many a fountain, a holy remnant kept for us by Beuno and Winefred. Under rain or dew, you will hardly find a country beneath heaven which is so luxuriant. Weak water brings a faithful testimony to our vale, but man bears no such witness. The old earth, in its appearance, shows an eternal share of virtue; it is only the human element that is faulty; it is man alone that is backward. Father, from thy hand will issue a spring from which will flow the beautiful prime good. Thou bringest by faith a sweet healing, the nourishment of religion; and Wales even now

134

will see true saints – pure, holy, virgin.
   Brân Maenefa sang this / April the twenty-fourth 1876.

A year later, Hopkins would express similar thoughts about the virtue of the countryside compared with the impiety of its inhabitants: 'Lovely the woods, waters, meadows, combes, vales, / All the air things wear that build this world of Wales; / Only the inmate does not correspond' ['In the Valley of the Elwy'].

Despite the alliteration 'Moonrise June 19 1876' is a very different kind of poetry to either 'The Wreck of the Deutschland' or 'The Silver Jubilee':

> I awoke in the midsummer not-to-call night, in the white and the walk of the morning:
> The moon, dwindled and thinned to the fringe of a fingernail held to the candle,
> Or paring of paradisaical fruit, lovely in waning but lustreless,
> Stepped from the stool, drew back from the barrow, of dark Maenefa the mountain;
> A cusp still clasped him, a fluke yet fanged him, entangled him, not quit utterly.
> This was the prized, the desirable sight, unsought, presented so easily,
> Parted me leaf and leaf, divided me, eyelid and eyelid of slumber.

Cut off from distractions and irrelevances by being alone in his room at night, the poet lays himself open to experience the moonrise in such a concentrated way, that even while one part of him finds perfect objective descriptions of the moon's appearance, to a more imaginative part the moon assumes a mythic persona and enacts a drama with the mountain Maenefa. This is poetry of joy and promise – written before Hopkins knew that 'The Wreck of the Deutschland' had been rejected – free-ranging exploration of the senses, as is 'The Woodlark', written a fortnight later, with its vivid description of poppies:

> The blood-gush blade-gash
> Flame-rash rudred
> Bud shelling or broad-shed
> Tatter-tangled and dingle-a-dangled
> Dandy-hung dainty head.

After the terrible disappointment of knowing that he would probably never see in print 'The Wreck of the Deutschland', into whose composition he had invested so much hope and time, Hopkins withdrew for a while from active composition; and it was not until the end of February next year, 1877, that poetry of his again appeared. The size and scope has now become severely curtailed. These are not poems carefully considered over a long period at the table in his room up in Mansions Gallery; both 'God's Grandeur' and 'The Starlight Night' are traditional sonnets, whose rhythms and rhyme-schemes every nineteenth-century poet would have in his head, and be able to bring to the surface whenever needed. The sonnet-form had been second nature to Hopkins while he was an Oxford undergraduate – in the two months from the end of April to June 1865 he had written ten sonnets and started others. Sonnets could be constructed in the head and memorised on a recreation-day or half-holiday walk into the Denbighshire countryside, once the wintry weather had lifted.

At the end of February 1877 there were bitter north winds on Maenefa and a very sharp frost. Hopkins was preparing for an examination, 'going over moral theology over and over again and in a hurry', finding that this 'most wearisome work' left him so tired that at the end of the day he was 'good for nothing' (L3, 143). And, contrary to his mother's wishes, he had been fasting over Lent, though only once a week, and, always puny looking, was losing weight. But the first primroses could be seen, and then, on the first day of the new month, the wind changed.

On 23 February, Hopkins wrote 'God's Grandeur', probably in reaction against the mind-set of his official studies, or, as he put it (L3, 144), 'in a freak' (the relevant OED definition is 'a capricious humour, notion, whim, or vagary'). This is the version he sent to his mother:

> The world is charged with the grandeur of God.
>   It will flame out, like shining from shook foil;
>   It gathers to a greatness, like an oozing oil
> Pressed. Why do men then now not fear His rod? –
> Generations have hard trod, have hard trod;
>   And all is seared with trade; bleared, smeared with toil;

And bears man's smudge and wears man's smell. The soil
Is barren; nor can foot feel, being shod.

And, for all this, nature is never spent;
    There lives the dearest freshness deep down things;
And though the last lights from the black West went
    O morning, on the brown brink eastwards, spring –
Because the Holy Ghost over the bent
    World broods with warm breast and with ah! bright wings.

As in the 'Cywydd', man and nature are compared. Commonly used in his time in descriptions of the Alps and the gothic style of architecture, two objects which Hopkins deeply revered for their combination of aesthetic and moral perfection, 'grandeur' implies transcendent greatness, and intrinsic qualities, as well as something magnificent to the eye. Without too much guesswork, it is possible to see how the poem arose from Hopkins's situation at the end of February. Wearily preoccupied with his moral theology, over and 'over and over again', he feels disgust at ordinary men who are unable to extricate themselves from the traditional common round of automaton toil, in which 'all is seared with trade', and 'bleared, smeared with toil'. 'Man's smudge' and 'smell' seem to have over-powered and tyrannised the ground, so that it appears barren. And humans are no longer in sentient contact with the soil, interposing shoes. (Hopkins often complained of shoes, their discomfort and unnaturalness, romantically admiring, at different times, the bare feet of bathers, children in the west of Ireland, and Maori foot-ballers.)

There is also in 'God's Grandeur' something redolent of indoor winter study, and the resulting limited perspective, in the first part of the poem – the countryside for many miles around St Beuno's was emphatically *not* 'seared with trade' nor 'smeared with toil', and Hopkins's joyful relationship with it was based on its predom-inantly *natural* characteristics, and the *lack* of human desecration. 'There lives the dearest freshness deep down things' suggests the cloistered priest's first surprise and delight at discovering an emer-gent primrose, 'the first rose' traditionally expressing winter dark-ness overcome, while the situation of the college on the steep valley-side looking across to the distant Snowdonian range had made it a place famous for observation of sunsets, from the roof of its central tower.

The poem also predicts the hope that will come with the joyful seasons later on that year, and the poetry that will ensue. A more immediate enthusiasm for nature, and also an implied human dullness, is expressed in 'The Starlight Night'. This is the version his mother received:

> Look at the stars! look, look up at the skies!
>   O look at all the fire-folk sitting in the air!
>   The bright boroughs, the glimmering citadels there!
> Look, the elf-rings! look at the out-round earnest eyes!
> The grey lawns cold where quaking gold-dew lies!
>   Wind-beat white-beam, airy abeles all on flare!
>   Flake-doves sent floating out at a farmyard scare!
> Ah well! it is a purchase and a prize.
>
> Buy then! Bid then! – What! – Prayer, patience, alms, vows.
> Look, look – a May-mess, like on orchard-boughs!
>   Look – March-bloom, like on mealed-with-yellow sallows!
>
> These are the barn, indeed: withindoors house
> The shocks. This pale and parclose hides the spouse
>   Christ and the mother of Christ and all His Hallows.

Hopkins had been 'much annoyed' that he had missed seeing the total eclipse of the moon at the end of February because 'someone on the spot' had not thought it worthwhile to tell people, and something of his exasperation comes out in this sonnet. The poet nudges the reader, who, he implies, is too dull to bother looking at the wonders of the night sky; up there, the poet can see in his imagination fire folk, boroughs, citadels, dewy lawns, silvery-leaved trees, and flake-feathered birds, and, in the sestet, a mess of orchard-blossom in May, or the bloom on sallows in March.

Vowed to poverty, he was unable to spend money on a gift for his mother's fifty-sixth birthday, so he intended to make fair copies of these two sonnets and send them to arrive at Oak Hill in time on 3 March. But his duties and studies did not allow him time to copy them out, and they did not reach her until two days after her birthday. She was so pleased with them that she had them framed, and for the rest of her life they hung over her bed, first at Hampstead, and then at Haslemere, where she would die in 1920, thirty-one years after her eldest son, but having had a copy of the first edition of his poems placed in her hands.

On his mother's birthday Hopkins passed the examination which qualified him to hear confessions. It was probably soon after that he wrote 'The Lantern out of Doors', a poignant account of his perennial loneliness:

> Sometimes a lantern moves along the night.
>   That interests our eyes. And who goes there?
>   I think; where from and bound, I wonder, where,
> With, all down darkness wide, his wading light?
>
> Men go by me, whom either beauty bright
>   In mould or mind or what not else makes rare:
>   They rain against our much-thick and marsh air
> Rich beams, till death or distance buys them quite.
>
> Death or distance soon consumes them: wind,
>   What most I may eye after, be in at the end
> I cannot, and out of sight is out of mind.
>
> Christ minds: Christ's interest, what to avow or amend
>   There, eyes them, heart wants, care haunts, foot follows kind,
> Their ransom, their rescue, and first, fast, last friend.

The previous year he had written to his mother about how 'very fatiguing' he found the annual postings, and their 'almost universal shift' of the Society's personnel: 'Much change is inevitable, for every year so many people must begin and so many more must have ended their studies.... Add deaths, sicknesses, leavings, foreign missions, and what not and you will see that ours can never be an abiding city nor any one of us know what a day may bring forth' (L3, 142). Jesuits were proud, he went on, of being 'ready for instant despatch', proving their subservience to their superiors' orders. But as in so many other details of Jesuit life, the cost in human feelings was ignored, and Hopkins's sufferings in this respect are well documented. One reason why he liked St Beuno's so much was that he was able to feel settled for – as he thought – four years; moves to other posts always affected him deeply.

One of his closest and most appreciative Jesuit friends, Francis Bacon, who had welcomed him to St Beuno's with a bunch of geraniums, had left the college some time ago, and some such severance may have been the immediate spur for this poem. The first eleven lines form a personal complaint about this elementary condition of the poet's life. In spite of the clear countryside atmosphere around him, he feels as though he is living in some miasma, 'our much-thick and marsh air', with the only relief the occasional intrusion of 'rare' men, of exceptional physical or mental frame, like a lantern in darkness (Hopkins here adapting Newman's famous image of the 'kindly light amid the encircling gloom'). With the image of the eye's movement there is also the self-pitying picture of the narrator remaining static, while having to watch the love-object travel directly and cruelly away from him. In contrast to the mental superiority to and conquest of the senses he is supposed to have from his training, Hopkins is saying that he absolutely depends on the physical for his happiness of mind.

The conclusion, the last three lines, forms some kind of official reaction to his complaint. But even if Christ does mind, even if his interest 'eyes them, heart wants, care haunts', it does not appear to provide, within the poem, a remedy for the narrator, who is stuck miserably in a constant, if occasionally light-interrupted, state of inner darkness and emotional deprivation. By using the metaphor of light and darkness, Hopkins had found a way of isolating and expressing a personal emotional problem; the discovery that he could create a poetic word-picture of a physical situation which truly represented his hidden emotional state must have been a heartening resource for him.

Another expression of nonconformity with his professional training comes in an untitled sonnet probably written within a month or so of 'The Lantern out of Doors':

> As kingfishers catch fire, dragonflies draw flame;
> As tumbled over rim in roundy wells
> Stones ring; like each tucked string tells, each hung bell's
> Bow swung finds tongue to fling out broad its name;
> Each mortal thing does one thing and the same:
> Deals out that being indoors each one dwells;

Selves – goes its self; *myself* it speaks and spells,
Crying *What I do is me: for that I came.*

I say more: the just man justices;
   Keeps grace: that keeps all his goings graces;
Acts in God's eye what in God's eye he is –
   Christ. For Christ plays in ten thousand places,
Lovely in limbs, and lovely in eyes not his
   To the Father through the features of men's faces.

Hopkins sympathised wholeheartedly with Duns Scotus's emphasis on apprehending an object by direct, sensuous perception of its individuality, rather than by a rational understanding of its essence. 'All things ... give off sparks and take fire, yield drops and flow, ring' (*S*, 195), Hopkins wrote in a spiritual note a few years later; and this poem urgently appeals for recognition of a higher moral status for sensuous intuition than the official scholastic Thomism allowed. (And on St George's Day 1877 he produced a poem supposed to honour the famous Dominican interpreter of Aquinas, Fr Thomas Burke, but actually attacking theologians who had supported Aquinas against Scotus; cunningly, he had written the poem in Latin, an obfuscating device he had used as an adolescent to prevent people from reading private notes he had made about his sexual impulses.)

The integrity of everything about a natural object is cleverly delineated in the opening violent images, where Hopkins gives the words denoting the typical actions of kingfishers and dragonflies the same component consonants as the objects themselves – thus 'kingfishers catch fire' and 'dragonflies draw flame'. The intrinsic properties of 'tucked string' and bell are also appropriately portrayed by complex sense- and sound-patterning. Somewhat predictably – given the octave's subject-matter – Hopkins is unable, however, to successfully extend his subject to 'the just man', who does not fit; and the last three lines stray again, forming another testimony to his susceptibility to human beauty, and a request that it be officially vindicated, because Christ is revealed in the loveliness of each individual.

*   *   *

In April Hopkins had a cold and a cough and was thinner, he thought, than he had ever been, but hoped 'to be all right with summer' (L3, 146). He was sent out for a ride in the pony-trap, a common prescription for Jesuits under the weather, and then, in the second week of May, to Rhyl, for a five-day holiday, 'for the good of his health' (as the house journal said). This seaside resort, visible in the far distance to the right from the terrace at the front of St Beuno's, was an early-Victorian construction to service railway-trippers seeking escape from Lancashire and Midlands industrial towns; its featureless beach and seasonal, terraced accommodation gave it a temporary and hollow appearance for most of the year.

It was not the ideal place for Hopkins to relax in, and with nothing to do but twiddle his thumbs he – not surprisingly – produced yet another poem contrasting the permanent grandeur and fresh beauty of nature's phenomena with the sordidness of man:

> *The Sea and the Skylark*
>
> On ear and ear two noises too old to end
>   Trench – right, the tide that ramps against the shore;
>   With a flood or a fall, low lull-off or all roar,
> Frequenting there while moon shall wear and wend.
>
> Left hand, off land, I hear the lark ascend,
>   His rash-fresh re-winded new-skeined score
>   In crisps of curl off wild winch whirl, and pour
> And pelt music, till none's to spill nor spend.
>
> How these two shame this shallow and frail town!
>   How ring right out our sordid turbid time,
>   Being pure! We, life's pride and cared-for crown,
>
> Have lost that cheer and charm of earth's past prime:
>   Our make and making break, are breaking, down
>   To man's last dust, drain fast towards man's first slime.

Unfortunately, walking on the Rhyl sands, without means of escape from the petty developers' architecture and shrill tourist vulgarities, Hopkins's disgust was evoked, especially in the last two lines, more than his sensitive reactions to the fresh beauty of the bird's song and movements. But the following weekend, back at St Beuno's, he began a five-day Whitsun holiday, and spent it walking in the burgeoning countryside, composing suitably celebratory poetry:

Spring

Nothing is so beautiful as Spring –
    When weeds, in wheels, shoot long and lovely and lush;
    Thrush's eggs look little low heavens, and thrush
Through the echoing timber does so rinse and wring

The ear, it strikes like lightnings to hear him sing;
    The glassy peartree leaves and blooms, they brush
    The descending blue; that blue is all in a rush
With richness; the racing lambs too have fair their fling.

What is all this juice and all this joy?
    A strain of the earth's sweet being in the beginning
In Eden garden. – Have, get before it cloy,

    Before it cloud, Christ, lord, and sour with sinning,
Innocent mind and Mayday in girl and boy,
    Most, O maid's child, thy choice and worthy the winning.

It is a scene not painted but vividly acted among a comparatively small number of details. Hopkins's words do not just picture, but evoke powerful movement. Some images convey more than normal perception: the blue is 'all in a *rush* with richness'. There is a progression in the mode and strength with which nature confronts the onlooker, from the weeds expressing their exuberantly sensuous character, to the hyperbolical comparison of the eggs and skies, to the excitement and violence of the thrush's vocal attack on the human ear.

But then the sestet opens with a question, 'What is all this juice and all this joy?', for which the reader is unprepared. The poet's moral training has caught up with him; he cannot enjoy (so he says) the pleasures of Spring, nor the reader the verbal expression of that enjoyment, unless those pleasures are placed within the perspective taught by Christian theology. And so Hopkins's priestly role comes into the poem, and he explains, gently and sweetly, the correct interpretation of Nature's beauty according to the Christian myth. However the dichotomy between the two kinds of language – the vivacious and sensuous word-painting of the octave, compared with the sestet's priestly explanation – tells another story, that of the two distinct parts of Hopkins's life. The intrusiveness of that question suggests a less than harmonious connection between the two, an imperfect synthesis.

Probably during the same Whitsun holiday Hopkins wrote one of his most perfect and rewarding poems:

The Caged Skylark

As a dare-gale skylark scanted in a dull cage,
    Man's mounting spirit in his bone-house, mean house, dwells –
    That bird beyond the remembering his free fells;
This in drudgery, day-labouring-out life's age.

Though aloft on turf or perch or poor low stage
    Both sing sometimes the sweetest, sweetest spells,
    Yet both droop deadly sometimes in their cells
Or wring their barriers in bursts of fear or rage.

Not that the sweet-fowl, song-fowl, needs no rest –
Why, hear him, hear him babble and drop down to his nest,
    But his own nest, wild nest, no prison.

Man's spirit will be flesh-bound, when found at best,
But uncumbered: meadow-down is not distressed
    For a rainbow footing it nor he for his bones risen.

It is not just a matter of the perfectly conceived and executed extended image, of aspiring man confined in his 'bone-house' compared to the wild skylark condemned to live out his days in a restricting cage, both sometimes bursting out in frustration or depressed and lifeless. It is also that the parable runs smoothly throughout the poem by means of a single voice. Whereas the two voices in 'Spring' represent opposed kinds of vision – the comparatively objective and unobjectionable sensuous view versus the subjective, ideological interpretation, whose credibility depends on the reader's preconceptions – there is the poet's single vision which unifies 'The Caged Skylark'.

This Whitsun holiday was one of the most poetically productive of Hopkins's life. This is probably the third sonnet he wrote in the four days:

In the Valley of the Elwy

I remember a house where all were good
    To me, God knows, deserving no such thing:
    Comforting smell breathed at very entering,
Fetched fresh, as I suppose, off some sweet wood.

That cordial air made those kind people a hood
    All over, as a bevy of eggs the mothering wing
    Will, or mild nights the new morsels of Spring:
Why, it seemed of course; seemed of right it should.

Lovely the woods, waters, meadows, combes, vales,
    All the air things wear that build this world of Wales;
    Only the inmate does not correspond.

God, lover of souls, swaying considerate scales,
Complete thy creature dear O where it fails,
    Being mighty a master, being a father and fond.

The house which the narrator recalls was that of the Watsons, at Shooter's Hill, on the border of Greenwich Park, in south-east London; so Hopkins wrote to Bridges, who had misunderstood the poem's argument, which was: 'As the sweet smell to those kind people so the Welsh landscape is NOT to the Welsh' (L1, 76). The figure at the start of the poem is like the narrator in 'The Lantern out of Doors', over-reacting to a too rare – but much needed – personal kindness: and the 'mothering wing' suggests the feminine presence and protectiveness which his mother had provided in his early years (he had been Kate Hopkins's favourite child), and which had been sadly lacking since then.

But the poet's argument is both incompletely stated and flawed, and it might not have been Bridges's fault that he failed to see it clearly. In the first part of the poem Hopkins is talking about a lovely house, whose cordiality emanated from two sources, one natural and the other human, which complemented each other. In the sestet, on the other hand, the lack in the Welsh of this correspondence (not a completely happy word here) is due not to the human failure in hospitality and welcome, but to their incorrect branch of religion. (I assume, both from Hopkins's idealistic picture of the Watsons, and from the fact that he unfortunately was in some ways unable to escape the unattractively dogmatic and unecumenical self-righteousness of so much Victorian religion, that the Shooter's Hill family was Roman Catholic). I cannot resist adding that the opposite of a homely welcoming house might be more readily seen as the institutional surroundings which were Hopkins's usual habitat in the Jesuits, rather than his Welsh neighbours.

'The Windhover' was probably the fifth poem that Hopkins wrote in May 1877. It was to be his favourite poem of this most poetically productive year, and of his 'salad days', his 'Welsh days'. (Though it was *not* the poem he liked best of all he wrote during his lifetime, as is often claimed.) It is a confident and mature poem, and behind it is his happiness at the best time of year, the joyful out-of-doors time, the lovely landscape, and his sense of achievement at his recent poetic fecundity; the next examination was in the distant future. In this poem – unlike nearly all the other Welsh poems – there is no lurking melancholy or unease, apart from 'my heart in hiding'; in fact there are no people except the narrator, alone in the Welsh countryside, open to experience, and encountering the falcon:

The Windhover

to Christ our Lord

I caught this morning morning's minion, king-
    dom of daylight's dauphin, dapple-dawn-drawn Falcon, in his
    riding
    Of the rolling level underneath him steady air, and striding
High there, how he rung upon the rein of a wimpling wing
In his ecstasy! then off, off forth on swing,
    As a skate's heel sweeps smooth on a bow-bend: the hurl and
    gliding
    Rebuffed the big wind. My heart in hiding
Stirred for a bird, – the achieve of, the mastery of the thing!

Brute beauty and valour and act, oh, air, pride, plume, here

Buckle! AND the fire that breaks from thee then, a billion
Times told lovelier, more dangerous, O my chevalier!

No wonder of it: sheer plod makes plough down sillion
Shine, and blue-bleak embers, ah my dear,
    Fall, gall themselves, and gash gold-vermilion.

Although Hopkins is commonly considered a Nature-poet – and
indeed a large proportion of both his poetry and his journals con-
cerns natural observations – his knowledge of neither flora nor
fauna was exceptionally extensive or deep, considering the widespread interest in both in Victorian Britain. (I am grateful to R.K.R.
Thornton for pointing this out to me.) He was always more interested in capturing in words the essence of the surface looks and
characteristic law or inscape of a natural object or phenomenon, and
did not possess more than a fairly basic ability to identify and name
common types. He doesn't seem to bother using common reference-
books, easily available to middle-class amateur observers in his day.
Sometimes this shows in, for example, his casual reference to a
whole species, rather than to a particular variety (the 'law of the
oak', a family with widely differing kinds and characteristics), or
mistaking, on the Isle of Man, a shag for a cormorant (a closely
related bird, but fairly easy to distinguish).

About the kestrel was a common bird, the most frequently
observed of the raptors, with widespread habitat, Hopkins did not
mention it before he came to Wales, nor afterwards. He captured or
'caught' a particular bird's performance one morning as though it
were the first time he had ever seen the most characteristic part of
its flight. In his poetic hands the bird becomes exotic and rare.

More than one book has suggested that Hopkins wrote the poem
after seeing a stuffed kestrel in a glass case which happened to be at
St Beuno's at the time: a theory too stupid and insensitive to be
taken seriously by anyone who has read Hopkins's words. It
shouldn't be necessary to say that the poem is about a living bird in
action and Hopkins's encounter with and observation of it.
Although it is still possible to see an occasional kestrel hunting on
Maenefa, they are more frequent near the Cwm road, the other side
of the Rhuallt crossroads, and an easy, short walk from St Beuno's.

In their search for small mammals, particularly voles, they usually hover at between twenty and forty feet from the ground, remaining stationary, with the tail spread in a fan and lowered, like a sort of stabilising rudder, while the wings flutter so rapidly that the bird appears motionless.

The extraordinarily long opening sentence and the breathless adjectival cluster 'the rolling level underneath him steady', together with the inescapable '-ing' rhyme in every line of the octave, represent the bird's sustained hover, and then the sweeping round which starts the glide. There is no let in the pressure of the narrative voice attacking the reader with live drama, imitating the paradox of the kestrel's apparent ecstasy, simultaneously static and tense. Hopkins was never better at achieving emotion, expression, meaning, and rhythm all at the same time: 'the rolling level underneath him steady air', 'how he rung upon the rein of a wimpling wing / In his ecstasy!'

'My heart in hiding' pictures the non-participant onlooker, Hopkins the poet, unable to take part in glorious activity or display or mingling, yet admiring and understanding what he himself cannot take part in, tense yet restrained by the barrier of the religious rule.

In the sestet, the chivalric imagery introduced by 'minion' and 'king-/dom ... dauphin' continues with Hopkins's lord, or 'chevalier' asked to buckle on, to use as armour, the various parts of the falcon's performance, 'brute beauty', 'valour', 'act', 'air', 'pride', and 'plume', so that, as the sun's reflected light would bounce off a knight's armour to dazzle everyone around, Christ would appear plainly in his full glory to all men. (The Jesuit motto and daily aim was 'to the greater glory of God'). And in the final three lines the two beautifully expressed images form a contrasting and magnificent ending, with Hopkins borrowing 'ah my dear' from his favourite poem by George Herbert known as 'Love (III)'.

* * *

To enable him to enter on his fourth and final year of theology at St Beuno's Hopkins needed three positive votes from the four professors who examined him on 22 July, but he received two low positive votes and two negative. He was one of four in the class of fourteen who failed and were not allowed to continue the course. Three days later he set out for a fortnight's holiday with his parents at Hampstead, and visited Bridges in Bloomsbury, making sure that Bridges had in safe-keeping copies of all the poems he had written up till now, in their latest versions, including 'The Wreck of the Deutschland'.

He then returned to St Beuno's to await news of where he would next be sent. 'Much against my inclination, I shall have to leave Wales', he told Bridges. 'No sooner were we among the Welsh hills', he wrote in a letter, 'than I saw the hawks flying and other pleasant sights soon to be seen no more' (*L3*, 146). One day, in Tremeirchion, he saw some of these pleasant sights, including the sky, the patchwork of fields, and colourful details of the vale's flora and fauna, and wrote a curtal (curtailed) sonnet celebrating his feelings:

> *Pied Beauty*
>
> Glory be to God for dappled things –
>   For skies of couple-colour as a brinded cow;
>   For rose-moles all in stipple upon trout that swim;
> Fresh-firecoal chestnut-falls; finches' wings;
>   Landscape plotted and pieced – folded, fallow, and plough;
>   And all trades, their gear and tackle and trim.
>
> All things counter, original, spare, strange;
>   Whatever is fickle, freckled (who knows how?)
>   With swift, slow; sweet, sour; adazzle, dim;
> He fathers-forth whose beauty is past change:
>   Praise him.

It is not just the the observer's joy at seeing these things that is celebrated here, but also the poet's skill at having conjured out of his perception the intrinsically correct, sole words which can do justice to the dappled things. But this is not the straightforward advocacy of Christian values which the poem's readers so often imagine, in spite of the orthodox frame of 'Glory be to God' at its start and 'Praise him' at the end. I think of the young James Joyce dutifully heading a heterodox, if not heretical, essay for his Jesuit schoolmasters 'A.M.D.G.' ('Ad maiorem Dei gloriam' – 'To the greater glory of God') and finishing it with 'L.D.S.' ('Laus Deo semper' – 'Praise be to God always').

'Pied Beauty' praises the *subjective* and the *aesthetic* and the *counter-orthodox*: the first six lines form a 'this-is-what-I-like' list, the contrast-patterns in nature (going back to the adolescent Hopkins's Ruskin-inspired journal) later in the nineteenth century enabled the Impressionists to energise their paintings by juxtaposing colours opposed in the spectrum, and, most importantly, the poet summarises his observation in the phrase 'All things counter, original, spare, strange'.

The vivid phrase, 'barbarous in beauty', in the opening line of the last poem Hopkins wrote before leaving Wales, is another example of pied beauty:

Hurrahing in Harvest

Summer ends now; now, barbarous in beauty, the stooks rise
Around; up above, what wind-walks! what lovely behaviour
Of silk-sack clouds! has wilder, wilful-wavier
Meal-drift moulded ever and melted across skies?

I walk, I lift up, I lift up heart, eyes,
Down all that glory in the heavens to glean our Saviour;
And, eyes, heart, what looks, what lips yet gave you a
Rapturous love's greeting of realer, of rounder replies?

And the azurous hung hills are his world-wielding shoulder
Majestic – as a stallion stalwart, very-violet-sweet! –
These things, these things were here and but the beholder
Wanting; which two when they once meet,
The heart rears wings bold and bolder
And hurls for him, O half hurls earth for him off under his feet.

'Hurrahing in Harvest' was, Hopkins said, 'the outcome of half an hour of extreme enthusiasm as I walked home alone one day [September 1st, 1877] from fishing in the Elwy' (*L*1, 56). 'A manic-depressive of a cyclothymic kind' was an eminent psychiatrist's first reaction to an account of Hopkins's mood-swings [letter to the present writer from William Sargant, author of *Battle for the Mind* etc.], and this poem's octave demonstrates him in ecstasy, with its egoistic assertion ('I walk, I lift up, I lift up'), exaggeration, exclamation, heightened emotions, and even the sexual involvement of the narrator – 'what lips yet gave you a/ Rapturous love's greeting of realer, of rounder replies?', where kisses, rather than words, are suggested.

The marvellous start, with the dropping cadence of 'Summer ends now' preparing for the upsurge of 'barbarous', is followed by the close but opposed association of the two parts of 'silk-sack', another example of counter-dapple. In the sestet other things from his pleasant-memories list are recalled (violets frequently occur in his prose-writings, and a stallion by which he felt attracted was mentioned in his undergraduate list of sins), before the sudden, artful calm of 'these things were here and but the beholder/ Wanting', which recalls the much clumsier 'only the inmate does not correspond' of 'In the Valley of the Elwy'.

Sometimes its ending is the weakest part of a Hopkins sonnet: he was usually better at individual observations than generalisations. But here there is no relaxation from the exaggerated images and exclamatory rhetoric; the intended climax succeeds, with a description of the ideal meeting between nature and its human beholder, when the poet's heart would – to use imagery from 'The Windhover' – finally leave its hiding-place.

This is not description of the scene but rather the poet deliciously savouring in his emotions a love-object. It is a poem where the heart (mentioned by name three times) is in charge. Many readers who follow him through his miserable times are grateful when they come across Hopkins in such obvious happiness.

Ten
'Summer ends now'

The first image in Schubert's 1827 song-cycle *Die Winterreise* ('The Winter Journey'), and the first word in lines one and two of its first song, 'Gute Nacht', is 'Fremd' – 'Stranger': 'A stranger came I hither, a stranger hence I go'. It is a reminder that Hopkins's imaginative summary of his past life in the 1885 sonnet, 'To seem the stranger lies my lot, my life/ Among strangers', was his personal and idiosyncratic version of a frequent image in a lore which had developed throughout nineteenth-century Europe, that of the Wanderer, the embittered outcast wandering through an alien landscape, unable to find rest.

The culmination of Hopkins's alienation is expressed in his desolate Dublin sonnets of 1885 and in the final three poems of 1889, written within three months of his death. But in fact throughout the twenty-odd years of Hopkins's maturity, from the mid-1860s to the late 1880s, he attempted to explore and define his troubled mental journey through life. The poetry Hopkins had composed while a student at Oxford is liberally sprinkled with pessimistic images, of disillusion, seasonal decay in nature, and malign fate, which anticipate the black despair pictured in the poems he wrote in Ireland. Sometimes in his undergraduate poetry negative images arise from human sympathy with nature's seasonal decay: 'So late there is no force in sap or blood' (in the poem 'Now I am minded'); at other times nature itself seems to be malevolent without reason: 'the dismal morn/ Into his hollow'd palm should moan the blast;/ And in grey bands the sun should lie still born' (in the lines starting 'Why if it be so'), or unseasonal: 'See how Spring opens with disabling cold'

– Hopkins's adult life seems fraught with complaints of how Spring was unSpringlike. In one Oxford poem, 'The Summer Malison', a divine curse is seen to be the cause of everything in the summer scene appearing to contradict pleasant expectations:

> Maidens shall weep at merry morn,
> And hedges break, and lose the kine,
> And field-flowers make the fields forlorn,
> And noonday have a shallow shine,
> And barley turn to weed and wild.

The tone and subject here is very similar to that of the Dublin fragment 'Strike, churl' ('heltering hail/ May's beauty massacre', and 'Bid joy back, have at the harvest, keep Hope pale'). Even the apparently innocuous act of looking at benign nature can lead inevitably to pessimism: 'Distance/ Dappled with diminish'd trees/ Spann'd with shadow every one'; and 'Bright hues long look'd at thin, dissolve and fly:/ Who lies on grass and pores upon the sky/ Shall see the azure turn expressionless'.

As in *Die Winterreise* Hopkins at Oxford can despair to such a degree that in madness he welcomes the most inhospitable places in nature: 'Then sweetest seems the houseless shore,/ Then free and kind the wilderness'. The unanswered pleas to God in 1885, such as 'Comforter, where, where is your comforting?', are first put in the poem written twenty years earlier 'My prayers must meet a brazen heaven', and in the 1866 'Nondum': 'God, though to Thee our psalm we raise/ No answering voice comes from the skies'. The pathos of the Dublin observation 'Birds build, but not I build' is anticipated in a poem written at Oxford in September 1865: 'Trees by their yield/ Are known; but I – / My sap is sealed,/ My root is dry'. In both Oxford and Dublin poems even death itself is sometimes welcome ('Nondum' and 'The times are nightfall').

From the time Hopkins took his first vows as a Jesuit there is the constant sense of his trying to find poetic vocabulary to define his hidden life, and 'stranger' in his 1885 poem is almost the culmination ('Time's eunuch', in 'Justus quidem tu es', is the final and lowest self-description). Before that he had discovered 'Fortune's football', taken from the title of a tale by Mrs Ogdon Meeker about a wandering outcast English Jesuit, and invented the phrase 'cobweb, soapsud, and frost-feather permanence', to describe his compulsory wandering, the constant shifting of his place of abode in the Jesuits (from 1877 to 1884 he was stationed at St Beuno's, Mount St Mary's, Stonyhurst, central London, Oxford, Bedford Leigh, Liverpool, Glasgow, Roehampton, Stonyhurst again, and Dublin – eleven places).

His three years at St Beuno's was halfway between his time as an Oxford student and his final period in Ireland. At first sight it might appear that he dealt most satisfactorily with the possibly divided allegiances to England and Wales. Deeply educated within and occupied with the English language he learned Welsh; he recharged poetic English with borrowings from Welsh language and poetic tradition. After his intimidated inspiration had been dormant and thin-blooded for some time, Wales became 'the Mother of Muses' to him. He had encouraged his Rector to encourage him in writing poetry as part of his job. He had pretended Welshness, invented himself as a Welshman.

But the fact was that the college was not Welsh. St Beuno's had been named by its founder, Fr Lythgoe, to signify a Welsh institution, or at least an institution in Wales. And yet it was part of the English province of the Society of Jesus, founded as replacement for the English Theologate previously situated at Stonyhurst, in Lancashire. The Clwyd valley had been chosen primarily for its unobrusiveness and remoteness, as the Jesuit order was still technically illegal under *10 George IV, Cap. 7.*, the so-called Emancipation Act; the Jesuit Theology course, says Bernard Basset (396), 'was not much affected by the countryside'. Hopkins was the only Jesuit at St Beuno's who knew any Welsh, and, as a result, there were next to no contacts with local people apart from those attending Mass. The buildings were recognisably English, designed by the architect of Birmingham Town Hall, who had also thought up the English urban hansom cab. Two of its prominent features, its strong, squat tower, and its fake portcullis, might be seen as referring to border-castles or strongholds of an alien culture surrounded by wild natives; both were inorganic and somewhat theatrical. And although the college was placed in the countryside of various St Beuno's legends and remnants, it was still within easy walking distance of Offa's Dyke, the traditional emblem of border-country.

And Hopkins was not a Welshman; he remained stubbornly English. This Englishness, together with his lack of a constant and qualified Welsh teacher, protected him against conformity to the tyrannical Welsh poetic devices; instead he selected for his personal use the bits and altered versions of what suited him. His impatience and strongly egocentric will, which always precluded scholarly achievement in his adult life, enabled him to keep Welsh language and poetry exactly where he wanted it, at a convenient but non-bothersome distance.

Other positive qualities about his stay in Wales were his discovery of holy wells, which were of enormous symbolic significance to him, more so than any other comparable symbol in his life, and, of course, the countryside, of which he was blissfully appreciative, and which he had reasonably extensive opportunities to explore. The landscape around Tremeirchion became one of the three most important stretches of countryside in his life – the others being the Hopkinsian haunts of Oxfordshire and Devon which in some degree it resembled.

But the journal, letters, and, especially, the poetry Hopkins wrote at St Beuno's tell a more subtle story, of the borderer, or wanderer, as in Schubert's 'Frühlingstraum', with no fixed mental abode, dreaming of Nature and perfect love and poetry, but being cruelly woken up to the harsh realities of his daily round, and human surroundings of incomprehension, even hostility.

* * *

The eleven poems Hopkins had written in English at St Beuno's in 1877 can be divided into four groups forming different stages of one range of emotion, descending from idealism to disillusion:

group 1: 'The Starlight Night', 'The Windhover', 'Pied Beauty'.
group 2: 'As kingfishers catch fire', 'Spring', 'The Caged Skylark', 'In the Valley of the Elwy', 'Hurrahing in Harvest'.
group 3: 'God's Grandeur', 'The Sea and the Skylark'.
group 4: 'The Lantern out of Doors'.

The poems in the first group have the straightforward purpose of praising God for varied examples of his natural creation. On the surface they are theologically orthodox but also simplified, perhaps evasively so: man is scarcely mentioned, and so the poem avoids facing the Victorian problem of his relationship with nature. The poems picture an ideal unsullied because the degenerating forces have been kept off the canvas. The narrator's optimism is apparently undiluted, and yet unasked questions lurk in two of the three poems. Why is the falcon's performance acknowledged covertly by the 'heart in hiding', rather than openly by the whole man? Why is the narrator's voice in 'The Starlight Night' so forceful unless it is assumed to have an apathetic audience?

The second group of poems conveys the poet's wish for the as yet unachieved ideal meeting of nature and man; a large distance between the present state and the ideal is taken as fact. In 'Hurrahing in Harvest' Man's unawareness is shown by his absence from the natural scene where the acknowledgement could take place ('these things were here and but the beholder wanting'), although the possibility of a meeting in the future is celebrated ('when once they meet'); the 'just man', in 'As kingfishers catch fire', is an imitation of Christ, an ideal rather than a description, and, similarly, 'Man's spirit ... when found at best' ('The Caged Skylark') *will be* flesh-bound', in some future time. More straightforwardly, in the Elwy valley God's creature at present 'fails', and 'the inmate does not correspond' – the awkward and ugly expression conveying an additional degree of distance from the ideal meeting. In 'Spring' the clouding and souring processes are both inevitable and not too distant.

In group three nature and man are not only far apart, but the narrator in addition expresses his active disgust at man's degenerate condition. The possibility of reconciling the two is not there; man seems irredeemably lost ('Nor can foot feel being shod') after generations of decay away from the ideal relationship with nature. The narrator-figure in these two poems is deeply and sadly pessimistic about man's present state. The last five lines of the 'God's Grandeur' octave and the whole sestet of 'The Sea and the Skylark' are shaped into gradual descents of negative feelings, giving the effect of one pessimistic thought preying on another to increase the weight on the narrator. In both poems his negative thoughts triumph: 'The Sea and the Skylark' ends with a downward movement to an irretrievably low point – 'drain fast towards man's first slime', and in 'God's Grandeur' the incomprehending question of the purpose behind the gap between man and nature – 'Why do men then now not reck his rod?' – is unanswered.

In 'The Lantern out of Doors', by employing the metaphor of darkness to represent the usual condition of life for the narrator, Hopkins denies any sense of reality to both nature and man in general: the personal problem of the isolation and rare relationship of the narrator with other people has excluded the larger question. Emotions and movements of nature are irrelevant to the narrator's state, because they are the epitome of positive qualities and he feels himself negative: 'birds build – but not I build', as he expressed this state in a poem written in the late 1880s, a period of much deeper and unrelieved depression, ending in his death.

In the 1877 Welsh sonnets Hopkins's recognition of the joyfulness of uncorrupted nature throws into relief his loneliness and his misanthropy, while faced with the insoluble dilemma of the incompatibility of his daily professional life with his private poetic impulses and gifts. All these poems, even the happiest, picture an individual endeavouring to find joy in and make sense of and validate his aloneness when surrounded by puzzling disharmony and incomprehension; while our other biographical knowledge of Hopkins gives an opposed picture of him as member of a community with a group-purpose quite different to anything expressed in his St Beuno's poems.

He had entered a religious order known for the thoroughness of its control over its members because he felt himself unable to suppress, using only his natural free-will, his strongly volatile and dangerous temperament sufficiently to live a daily life satisfactory by the most scrupulous ethical standards of the 1860s. As masochistic as a George Eliot heroine, he had joined because he knew he was a 'blackguard', his individual exploratory nature opposed to the difficult communal discipline of the Jesuits. At times in his Jesuit career, particularly in its early stages, the more he felt himself falling short of successfully subordinating himself to the order's discipline, the more he wilfully chastened himself (as, for example, his six-months' self-imposed 'custody of the eyes', a horrific deprivation for a poet who largely relied on visual phenomena). But as time went by, and he accustomed himself to a degree of failure in his career, his natural rebelliousness asserted itself more, and – particularly in Dublin, where he felt justified by his patriotic conscience to oppose political tendencies and hence other teachings of some Irish co-religionists – his poetry developed a freedom from dogmatic control, to explore its author's inner life to a degree unthinkable earlier on.

Hopkins's St Beuno's poems show him in a fascinating intermediate stage. His three-year period in Wales starts with dull occasional verse, such as the first St Winefride poems, conforming to expected sentiment and displaying his self-suppression rather than self-expression, passes to 'The Wreck of the Deutschland', his greatest opportunity to demonstrate an achieved combination of objectively priestly and subjectively aesthetic purposes, and – the rejection having caused a reassessment – finishes with the subtly concealed rebellion of 'Pied Beauty' and 'Hurrahing in Harvest'.

The first Welsh poems, then, look backward to Hopkins's uninspired occasional poems written in the early eighteen-seventies at Stonyhurst, while the final ones anticipate the remarkably fine, independent sonnets written in late-1880s Ireland. Generally speaking, the optimistic and fruitful times of the St Beuno's years provoked optimism and poetry, especially when Hopkins was free from professional duties and preoccupations.

Three weeks after composing 'Hurrahing in Harvest' Hopkins was ordained to the priesthood. But he was in pain, and was operated on, for circumcision, and took a fortnight to recover. On the morning of 19 October 1877 Hopkins took his last look at St Beuno's, and at Wales, and set out for Mount St Mary's College, near Sheffield, where, he wrote, the landscape is 'not very interesting' and the air 'never once clear'.

Bibliography

1. Works by Hopkins

Unless otherwise stated, poems are quoted from *Gerard Manley Hopkins* (The Oxford Authors), edited by Catherine Phillips (Oxford, 1986), which is cited in text as *P*.

J. The Journals and Papers of Gerard Manley Hopkins, edited by Humphry House and Graham Storey (London, 1959).

L1 The Letters of Gerard Manley Hopkins to Robert Bridges, edited by C.C. Abbott (London, 1955).

L2 The Correspondence of Gerard Manley Hopkins and Richard Watson Dixon, edited by C.C. Abbott (London, 1955).

L3 The Further Letters of Gerard Manley Hopkins, edited by C.C. Abbott (London, 1956).

S. The Sermons and Devotional Writings of Gerard Manley Hopkins, edited by C. Devlin (London, 1959).

2. Other works cited in text

Borrow   George Borrow, *Wild Wales: Its people, language and scenery* (London, 1862).

Clarke   R.F. Clarke, 'The Training of a Jesuit', *Nineteenth Century*, x1 (August 1896), 211-25.

Defoe   Daniel Defoe, *A Tour through the Whole Island of Great Britain* (London, 1724-6; 1971 edition), letter 6 ('The West and Wales').

DRT   Ven. D.R. Thomas, *The History of the Diocese of St. Asaph* (Oswestry: Caxton Press, 1874), new edition 1908-13.

Flora   Richard Mabey, *Flora Britannica* (London, 1996).

HRB   *Hopkins Research Bulletin.*
HTJ   Alfred Thomas SJ, *Hopkins the Jesuit: the Years of Training* (London, 1969).
Hunter   [Sylvester Hunter SJ,] *'St Beuno's'*, *Letters and Notices* [private Society of Jesus publication] 26 (1901), 43.
Lahey   G.F. Lahey, *Gerard Manley Hopkins* (London, 1930).
LvN   L.M. van Noppen, 'Gerard Manley Hopkins: The Wreck of the Deutschland' (doctoral thesis, University of Gröningen, 1980).
OED   *Oxford English Dictionary.*
OM   Denis Meadows, *Obedient Men* (New York, 1954).
W   Norman White, *Hopkins: A Literary Biography* (Oxford, 1992).

3. Selection of other works used

Attwater, Donald, *A Dictionary of Saints* (London, 1938).
Attwater, Donald, *The Catholic Church in Modern Wales* (London, 1935).
Basset, Bernard, S.J., *The English Jesuits From Campion to Martindale* (London, 1967).
Blundell, Margaret and Agnes, *St Winefride and her Holy Well* (London, 1954).
Bremer, Rudolph, 'Gerard Manley Hopkins: The Sonnets of 1865' (doctoral thesis, University of Gröningen, 1978).
Burnham, Helen, *A Guide to Ancient and Historic Wales: Clwyd and Powys* (London, 1995).
Butler, Rev. Alban, *The Lives of the Primitive Fathers, Martyrs, and other Principal Saints*, volume xi (third edition, 1799), 71-80 (for story of Saint Winefride, V.M.).
Charles-Edwards, T.M., *Saint Winefride and Her Well* (London, 1962).
Charles-Edwards, T.M., (ed.), *Two Mediaeval Welsh Poems: Stori Gwenfrewi A'I Ffynnon by Tudur Aled and Ffynnon Wenfrewi* (Aberdovey, 1971).
Culwick, Colin, *Oh! I Do Like to be Beside the Seaside: Memories of Rhyl* (Rhyl, n.d.).
David, Christopher, *St Winefride's Well: A History and Guide* (Slough, 1971).
Davis, William, *Handbook for the Vale of Clwyd* (Ruthin, 1856, repr. Clwyd, 1988).

Feeney, Joseph J., SJ, 'Grades, Academic Reform, and Manpower: why Hopkins never completed his course in theology', *Hopkins Quarterly* 9(1) (Spring 1982).

Gardner, W.H., *Gerard Manley Hopkins: A Study of Poetic Idiosyncrasy in Relation to Poetic Tradition* (two volumes, London, 1966), particularly volume 2, pages 143-58, on Welsh influences on Hopkins.

Gardner, W.H., 'G. Manley Hopkins as a Cywyddwr', *Transactions of the Honourable Society of Cymmrodorion*, session 1940-41, 184-8.

Grigson, Geoffrey, *The Englishman's Flora* (London, 1975).

Grigson, Geoffrey, comp., *The English Year* (Oxford, 1967).

Grigson, Geoffrey, *Wild Flowers in Britain* (London, 1944).

Holland, Richard, *Supernatural Clwyd: The Folk Tales of North-East Wales* (Llanrwst, 1989).

Hoskins, W.G., *English Landscapes* (London, 1973).

House, Madeline, and House, Humphry, 'Books Belonging to Hopkins and his Family', *HRB* 5 (1974), 34-5.

Hubbard, Edward, *The Buildings of Wales: Clwyd (Denbighshire and Flintshire)* (Harmondsworth, 1986).

Jones, David, *Letters to a Friend*, ed. Aneirin Talfan Davies (Swansea, 1980).

Jones, Francis, *The Holy Wells of Wales* (Cardiff, 1954).

Keane, F., SJ, 'St Beuno's, 1848-1948', *Letters and Notices* 56 (1948), 191-2.

Lilly, Gweneth, 'Welsh Influence in the Poetry of Gerard Manley Hopkins', *Modern Language Review* 38 (July 1943),192-205.

Mackenzie, Norman H., (ed.), *The Poetical Works of Gerard Manley Hopkins* (Oxford, 1990).

Maxwell-Scott, M.M.C., *Henry Schomberg Kerr: Sailor and Jesuit* (London, 1901).

Roberts, Dewi, (ed.), *A Clwyd Anthology* (Bridgend, 1995).

Roberts, Dewi, (ed.), *Visitors' Delight: An Anthology of Visitors' Impressions of North Wales* (Llanrwst, 1992).

Thomas, Alfred, SJ, 'Hopkins, Welsh and Wales', *Transactions of the Honourable Society of Cymmrodorion*, session 1965, pt.II (1966), 272-85.

Thornton, R.K.R., (ed.), *All My Eyes See: the Visual World of Gerard Manley Hopkins* (Sunderland, 1975).

Weyand, Norman, SJ (ed.), *Immortal Diamond: Studies in Gerard Manley Hopkins* (London, 1949).

Series Afterword

The Border country is that region between England and Wales which is upland and lowland, both and neither. Centuries ago kings and barons fought over these Marches without their national allegiance ever being settled. It is beautiful, gentle, intriguing, and often surprising. It displays majestic landscapes, which show a lot, and hide some more. People now walk it, poke into its cathedrals and bookshops, and fly over or hang-glide from its mountains, yet its mystery remains.

The subjects covered in the present series seem united by a particular kind of vision. Writers as diverse as Mary Webb, Dennis Potter and Thomas Traherne, painters and composers such as David Jones and Edward Elgar, and writers on the Welsh side such as Henry Vaughan and Arthur Machen, bear one imprint of the border woods, rivers, villages and hills. This vision is set in a special light, a cloudy, golden twilight so characteristic of the region. As you approach the border you feel it. Suddenly you are in that finally elusive terrain, looking from a bare height down on to a plain, or from the lower land up to a gap in the hills, and you want to explore it, maybe not to return.

There are more earthly aspects. From England the border meant romantic escape or colonial appropriation; from Wales it was roads to London, education or employment. Boundaries are necessarily political. Much is shared, yet different languages are spoken, in more than one sense. The series authors reflect the diversity of their subjects. They are specialists or academics; critics or biographers; poets or musicians themselves; or ordinary people with however an established reputation of writing imaginatively and directly about what moves them. They are of various ages, both sexes, Welsh and

English, border people themselves or from further afield.

The three years Gerard Manley Hopkins spent at St Beuno's College in the Elwy Valley near Offa's Dyke, in final preparation for the Catholic priesthood, were a triple *annus mirabilis* which yielded all that he is usually most remembered for. The great harvest included 'God's Grandeur', 'Spring', 'The Windhover' and 'Pied Beauty'; some pieces only slighly less favourably thought of like 'Penmaen Pool', 'The Starlight Night' and 'As kingfishers catch fire'; and of course the epochal longer poem which re-started it all and- which equally, if in hindsight, inaugurated poetic modernism itself, 'The Wreck of the Deutschland'. Hopkins's crossing of the border into Wales, into the priesthood and (back) into poetry itself, led to intricacies of joy, conflict and poetic and verbal innovation in which each new generation of readers finds a new challenge. In unravelling these intricacies, the poet's major biographer Norman White reveals in unique detail the nature of this extraordinary turning-point in the history of poetry in English in Wales and, of course, far beyond.

Index

INDEX

About the Author

Educated at the universities of London and Liverpool, Norman White is Senior Lecturer in Modern English Literature at University College, Dublin. Among the foremost Hopkins scholars, his *Hopkins: A Literary Biography* (OUP) won the Dictionary of Literary Biography Prize and was shortlisted for the Whitbread Biography Prize.

The Border Lines Series

Elizabeth Barrett Browning Barbara Dennis

Bruce Chatwin Nicholas Murray

The Dymock Poets Sean Street

Edward Elgar: Sacred Music John Allison

Margiad Evans: Ceridwen Lloyd-Morgan

Eric Gill & David Jones at Capel-y-Ffin Jonathan Miles

A.E. Housman Keith Jebb

Herbert Howells Paul Spicer

Francis Kilvert David Lockwood

Arthur Machen Mark Valentine

Wilfred Owen Merryn Williams

Edith Pargeter: Ellis Peters Margaret Lewis

Dennis Potter Peter Stead

John Cowper Powys Herbert Williams

Philip Wilson Steer Ysanne Holt

Henry Vaughan Stevie Davies

Mary Webb Gladys Mary Coles

Samuel Sebastian Wesley Donald Hunt

Raymond Williams Tony Pinkney

Francis Brett Young Michael Hall